VARIETIES OF LIBERALISM
IN CENTRAL AMERICA

Varieties of Liberalism in Central America

NATION-STATES AS WORKS IN PROGRESS

Forrest D. Colburn and Arturo Cruz S.

UNIVERSITY OF TEXAS PRESS
Austin

Requests for permission to reproduce material from this
work should be sent to:
    Permissions
    University of Texas Press
    P.O. Box 7819
    Austin, TX 78713-7819
    www.utexas.edu/utpress/about/bpermission.html

∞ The paper used in this book meets the minimum
requirements of ANSI/NISO Z39.48-1992 (R1997) (Permanence of Paper).

Library of Congress Cataloging-in-Publication Data
Colburn, Forrest D.
    Varieties of liberalism in Central America : nation-
states as works in progress / Forrest D. Colburn and
Arturo Cruz S.—1st ed.
        p.   cm.
    Includes bibliographical references.
ISBN 978-0-292-71720-6 (cloth : alk. paper)—
ISBN 978-0-292-71721-3 (pbk. : alk. paper)
    1. Central America—Politics and government—
1979– . 2. Liberalism—Central America.   I. Cruz S.,
Arturo J. (Cruz Sequeira).   II. Title.
    JL1410.C64 2007
    320.5109728—dc22
                                          2007000698

CONTENTS

ACKNOWLEDGMENTS

We are colleagues at INCAE, Latin America's premier graduate school of management. (Initially, INCAE was an acronym, but now it is the formal—and only—name of the institute.) Our work at INCAE has led us both to travel frequently throughout Central America, speaking to a diverse set of individuals, about an equally varied set of issues. Sometimes our work has overlapped, but even when it has not, it has been complementary. We have garnered a wealth of information and impressions. For such a wide-ranging study, though, we also draw on more prosaic experiences in the countries of the isthmus. And some of our most impressionable experiences date back to the heady turmoil of the 1980s. Memory has a murky but indelible role in scholarship.

Those at INCAE's campus in La Garita, Costa Rica, who facilitated our research and writing include Roberto Artavia, Tom Bloch, Esteban Brenes, and Arturo Condo. Helpful comments on drafts of the work were offered by Herb Broderick, Consuelo Cruz, Lowell Gudmundson, John Ickis, Andrea Prado, Pedro Raventós, Luis Rivera, Norman Uphoff, and Ralph Lee Woodward. Help with photographs was provided by Celeste González in Managua, José Zúñiga in San José, and Spencer Throckmorton in New York. *Estamos agradecidos.*

Every sentence I utter must be understood not as an affirmative, but as a question.
—NIELS BOHR

INTRODUCTION

Why do some countries progress while others seemingly so similar stagnate? What explains abrupt changes in the tack of countries? Why does adversity strengthen some countries and weaken other countries? Probing deeper, in this era of unprecedented movement of people, goods, and ideas, just what constitutes a country, a state, a nation?

These sweeping questions have been suggested to us by watching the evolution of the five countries of the Central American isthmus. In the 1980s, Nicaragua, El Salvador, and Guatemala were wrecked by civil war, unnerving Honduras and Costa Rica. The violence was deemed by many to be an inevitable consequence of stark class divisions and a subordinate position in the international economy. The United States was blamed, too, for contributing to the permanence of an ill-suited status quo. These determinants of political fate were widely viewed as so immutable, so ponderous, that there was judged to be no middle ground between bloody revolution and bloody repression.

A quarter of a century later—a long period in the life of an individual, but a short period in the life of a country—the region looks different, and it is different. The salience of class has receded, remarkably so, and political violence is rare. Insurgents have vanished, and so—even—have many organizations of the poor and the dispossessed. The military, long such a force in Guatemala, Honduras, El Salvador, and Nicaragua, has receded from political life. In all five countries of the region, governors are chosen in free, competitive elections. And in these elections,

Central Americans have embraced political moderation and continuity. The results of these elections have been accepted as sacrosanct by all political actors.

Another sea change is in the perception of the international economy, formerly feared; it is now seen as a neutral arena to be entered valiantly. And the behemoth, the United States, has come to be home to many Central Americans, a cultural beacon, and a commercial partner actively courted by governors of the region's countries.

How did the five Central American countries alter course so quickly and so uniformly? Why the ascendancy of liberalism, of democracy and unfettered markets? There are, to be sure, rough edges—inconsistencies, some of them glaring—in this change of tack. But the change is nonetheless remarkable. Where is this new paradigm, interpreted as it is within the confines of individual nation-states, taking Central Americans?

Within the puzzle of how Central Americans have changed course lies an enigma, one that bedevils efforts to explain economic—and so, social—development. While all of the five countries of the isthmus have remade themselves since the 1980s, one country has truly prospered—moved forward. Another country, unfortunately, has stumbled backwards. In the 1960s, neighboring Nicaragua and Costa Rica had comparable per capita incomes. The World Bank's *World Development Report 2005* suggested Costa Rica had reached an awkward milestone: its per capita income was reported to be six times that of Nicaragua. What went right? What went wrong? How can such dissimilar outcomes within such a compressed period of time be explained?

Costa Rica's success and Nicaragua's misfortune is more than an enigma. Most Costa Ricans live reasonably well, and the percentage of Costa Ricans mired in poverty has declined significantly since the 1980s. In contrast, most Nicaraguans are overwhelmed with poverty and hardship; life has gotten "harder." Why should "citizenship" matter so much? What does it mean, anyway, to be "Costa Rican," "Nicaraguan," or, for that matter, "Salvadoran," "Honduran," or "Guatemalan"?

We have so many expansive, searching questions. And the academy today does not encourage—or welcome—asking big questions, believing they cannot be answered with certainty. It is true; we can offer only tentative answers. Indeed, a leitmotiv of the study is the indeterminacy of the fate—the politics—of countries. There is causality, but not the kind that can be revealed in the laboratory or on the blackboard. There are simply too many "variables," and they cannot be isolated or measured, and, moreover, they interact in a dizzy, obfuscating way. Countries are enigmatic.

Still, the nation-state is the most important political entity. Furthermore, the differences among nation-states, even those that are neighbors, can be striking. Such is the case in Central America. In looking for answers to questions about the evolution of countries and the differences among them, attention can be drawn to the constraints nation-states face and the quirks of fortune. More intriguing are the more malleable national idiosyncrasies—buried in culture—and the choices of local political actors.

Combing through the recent history of the five Central American republics offers a reminder of the many constraints nation-states confront, including those of economic trends emanating from far afield. There is also fortune, good and bad. A paired comparison of Nicaragua and Costa Rica, though, underscores the considerable weight of local decisions, in particular of the kinds and quality of public institutions built, and of the investments made (or not made) in social services. These decisions, in turn, shape the ability of state and society to respond to the exigencies of the international economy, fashions in ideology, and the quirks of fortune. Furthermore, good decisions lead to opportunities: there is momentum in economic development. (But likewise, poor decisions have opportunity costs.)

While local choices matter, it is not always clear who makes them—or when and how they are made. It is easy, but often facile, to point to towering political figures who make what appear to be transcendental decisions at moments of crisis, at what may appear to be critical junctures. Maybe leaders are hemmed into making decisions. Maybe they make calculations of personal gain. Alternatively, maybe their decisions reflect deeply ingrained, idiosyncratic cultural norms. For example, the differences between investments made in public education in Nicaragua and Costa Rica are striking and appear, over the course of decades, to have contributed to the divergence in welfare between the two countries. An anecdote about Anastasio Somoza, the Nicaraguan dictator, recounts how in the 1960s he responded to the suggestion of a foreign aid official that Nicaragua spend more on education by asking, "If everyone goes to school, who will pick the coffee?" Was Somoza speaking, or was he simply a mouthpiece for the upper echelon of a society divided by class? It is unclear. Was there ever one—identifiable—decision made in Nicaragua to limit spending on public education? Surely not. Tracing the trajectory of political decisions in Costa Rica—and of the other three countries of the region—is likewise elusive.

The deeper one probes into individual nation-states, the more cautious one is about generalizing and the less faith one has in theories about politics. Instead, questions spew forth. In our efforts to answer, cautiously and honestly, some of the more pertinent questions, we hope to sketch a fair portrait of Central America in its present incarnation. Good questions can narrate descriptive detail just as well as can a single-minded hypothesis.

A sobering conclusion that emerges from the study is that liberalism has no inherent determinants. Liberalism is in vogue: since the turmoil of the 1980s all of the countries of Central America have embraced democracy and unfettered markets. But, again, there are no inherent determinants for what liberalism offers a polity. Democracy and unfettered markets, when welded to the messy realities of individual countries, are compatible with many different outcomes. There are thus many varieties of liberalism. The world is more pluralistic in both causes and effects than either academic theories or political rhetoric suggest.

While delineating trends in Central America, we also hope to contribute, if only modestly, to a renewed appreciation for the study of countries. The influence of the nation-state always needs to be acknowledged. In politics, context is important and so geography matters.

VARIETIES OF LIBERALISM
IN CENTRAL AMERICA

ENIGMATIC
NATION-STATES AND
CONCEPTUAL NIHILISM

In William Shakespeare's play *Twelfth Night or What You Will*, Viola survives a shipwreck—"our ship did split." Once washed ashore she asks, "What country, friends, is this?... Who governs here?" These two questions are timeless. The nation-state—the country—remains the locus of most important political decisions. And these decisions are made by governors, exercising control over the state.

The nation-state is the most consequential unit of analysis in politics. Politicians know this; readers of newspapers know it. Surprising, then, is the limp interest in individual nation-states by students of politics. Those in the academy who study politics have long been drawn to theory. And the generation of theory comes from studying recurring political behavior. In the most extreme conceptualization, nothing in politics is held to be unique; thus, it is ignoble (or at least risky) to study subjects that lead to this theoretical dead-end, to what can only be description of a particular case. However, there is a high cost to ignoring the specific context of politics, including prominently the individual nation-state that provides the arena for much give-and-take. Theory can never be that useful, that relevant, if it skirts the messy, idiosyncratic settings in which it is conducted.

Sadly, the slighting of individual cases easily leads to a reification of politics. A colleague at Princeton University, Atul Kohli, deadpans: "I work on India, a country with a population of one billion, and I am always asked about 'the larger significance' of my work." The quip is uttered in frustration as well as irony. The larger significance is theory. Indians—their cares and needs—are just data.

Kohli nonetheless presses forward, writing with verve about India. Others, too, risk—or accept—intellectual marginalization by studying individual countries (or regions of the world). There is a variety of country studies. Some make an effort to apply a theoretical concept to an individual case. Other works try to unravel a sticky political problem, such as, perhaps, communal conflict. Still other works are histories of individual polities. There are, however, not well-established precepts or conceptual models for dissecting nation-states, for taking their measure. And, again, there is not much in the way of encouragement either for making an effort to understand the workings and the paths of specific countries.

Successive schools of political analysis do suggest some useful places to begin an inquiry into individual nation-states: history, social relations (including prominently class cleavages), the formation and behavior of political institutions, regime type, economic activity and linkages to international markets, elite behavior, political learning, and political culture. But this list is long, and there is no consensus on how to aggregate these variables or how to assign to them explanatory weights in the assessments of individual countries. Likewise, while there are long-standing definitions of "country," "nation," and "state," these tend to be at a high level of generality and so need to be cautiously refined when applied to specific cases.

Schools of political analysis come and go. There are fashions in political analysis in which one particular kind of explanation—or variable—is favored. But these fleeting schools of analysis are not cumulative—they do not build on one another. Instead, fashions of political analysis follow the political events—and political tenor—of their era.

An illuminating example is the life-cycle of "bureaucratic-authoritarianism." In 1964, Brazil had a military coup. Two years later, the military also seized power in neighboring Argentina. In 1973, democratic regimes collapsed in other economically advanced Latin American nations: Chile and Uruguay. That same

year, an Argentine, Guillermo O'Donnell, published a mono-graph at the Institute of International Studies of the University of California, Berkeley. The work was titled *Modernization and Bureaucratic-Authoritarianism: Studies in South American Politics.* The title suggested something new was afoot in the four most prosperous countries of South America. Instead of rule by individual and so personalistic military leaders, the military ruled as an institution. Correspondingly, the military adopted a technocratic, bureaucratic approach to making and implementing public policies. By joining the adjective bureaucratic with authoritarian, a new addition was made to the many typologies of national political regimes.

O'Donnell was not just adding a typology or describing a consequential series of political events in South America. He was more ambitious. He proposed an explanation, a theory, of why bureaucratic-authoritarianism emerged. O'Donnell posited an economic explanation for the rise of authoritarianism. He focused on Latin America's relatively "late industrialization" and the region's dependence on foreign capital, technology, and managerial expertise to promote industrialization. While Argentina and other similarly situated countries attained some initial success in producing consumer goods, the "deepening" of industrialization to include production of intermediate and capital goods ran afoul of the strictures of international capitalism. The inevitable economic crisis generated political tensions, including, for example, strikes, that were necessarily smothered by bureaucratic-authoritarianism.

Bureaucratic-authoritarianism gained intellectual popularity. The model was used to discuss Mexico, authoritarian though not under military tutelage, and the reformist military regimes of Peru and Ecuador. The concept of bureaucratic-authoritarianism was extended by some—at least for the purpose of contrast—to the more personalistic military rule common at the time in other, usually poorer countries of Latin America: Paraguay, Bolivia, Panama, Nicaragua, El Salvador, Honduras, and Guatemala. The model was even used for countries outside the region, including, for example, Egypt.

O'Donnell's conceptualization of bureaucratic-authoritarianism, based on the economically advanced countries of South America, was the most sophisticated of the many analyses of authoritarianism in Latin America. But O'Donnell was decidedly in step with intellectual fashion, which was to offer economic explanations—blaming international and domestic capitalism—for undesired political outcomes. A representative book from Central America from the era is Jaime Wheelock's *Nicaragua: Imperialismo y dictadura*, published in 1979 in Mexico City and reprinted the following year in Havana. Wheelock, one of the nine Sandinista *Comandantes de la Revolución*, argued forcefully that Nicaragua's dictatorship was the result of the machinations of international capitalism rolling over the supine local business elite. Perhaps ironically, Wheelock relied heavily for information on a dissertation submitted to the Harvard Business School in 1972 by Harry Strachan titled *The Role of Business Groups in Economic Development: The Case of Nicaragua*.

During the late 1970s and the 1980s, though, there was an unanticipated "wave" of democracy that washed away authoritarian regimes throughout Latin America. In country after country, authoritarian governments—usually military—gave way to constitutional rule, competitive party politics, elections, and civilian supremacy. The first Latin American country to make the transition to democracy was Ecuador in 1979, followed by its neighbor Peru in 1980. Argentina followed suit in 1983, as did Uruguay in 1984. In Central America, the military returned to the barracks in El Salvador in 1984; the military in neighboring Guatemala did the same in 1986. Dating the transition in Bolivia and Honduras is difficult, but in both countries, 1985 seems to have been a pivotal year. In 1989 Brazil finally jettisoned its military rule. Chile and Nicaragua changed regimes—embracing democracy—in 1990. Paraguay had open and competitive elections in 1993. Finally, Mexico, governed by the Institutionalized Revolutionary Party (the PRI) since 1929, began to "open" politically during this period, breaking the hegemony of this mild but hardly benign authoritarian regime. Latin America, which had only three well-established democracies during the dark years of the 1970s—Costa Rica, Venezuela, and Colombia—suddenly looked very different: the region was overwhelmingly committed to democracy.

Further confounding prevailing explanations of politics in the region, this transition took place during the most trenchant economic recession since the world depression of the 1930s. Perhaps most confusing, Mexico's lengthy transition to democracy took place as it opened itself economically to increased trade with the United States and Canada, through the North American Free Trade Agreement (NAFTA). The assertion that participation in the international economy was politically pernicious appeared unsustainable, as did, in fact, any assertion of a causal link between economic activity—or structure—and politics.

Indeed, the transition to democracy in Latin America was accompanied by another sweeping—and unexpected—change: the widespread adoption of market-based economic policies. Protective tariffs came tumbling down, as did barriers to foreign investment. Many state enterprises were sold; government subsidies and other market distortions were eliminated. Governments committed themselves to providing a stable macro-economic environment—prominently through the control of inflation—and left the rest up to the private sector. So, unexpectedly, liberal doctrine and practice came to reign in both government and in the economy: it was to be democracy and unfettered markets.

In the early 1990s, Guillermo O'Donnell, who achieved fame in academic circles through the diffusion of his work on bureaucratic-authoritarianism, began to report in public forums that he no longer believed in it. He disavowed it swiftly and completely. At one such gathering, at the Institute for Advanced Study in Princeton, he added that in his native Argentina he was taken with how people drive their cars, how quick they are to cut into lines at movie theaters, and how they treat their hired help. It is culture! The key question, he concluded, was "How do cultural practices become embedded in political institutions?"

Legions of scholars halted their explorations of why Latin America was destined to authoritarianism and began speaking and writing about the "transition to democracy." They worked hard, not to explain the fate of individual countries, but instead to develop theories that would hold across cases, even span geographical and cultural regions: Latin America, Southern Europe (in particular Portugal, Spain, and Greece), and later, after 1989, Eastern Europe. What was quickly buried in the bowels of libraries was not so much the typology of bureaucratic-authoritarianism, but instead the explanatory baggage that had accompanied its presentation and embellishment: the link between economic development—"late industrialization," "formation of the urban proletariat," "foreign multinationals," "declining terms of trade," and the like—with political outcomes. Sure, economic structures and activity influence politics, but it was suddenly untenable to argue that there was an ironclad relationship between the two spheres.

The many articles and books about the transition to democracy in Latin America and elsewhere are thoughtful. They offer numerous insights and a few plausible generalizations—though despite the pretensions of theory, the literature has never managed to attain any predictive utility. However, with the passage of years, and not very many at that, it has become increasingly evident that there is no universal paradigm of transition to democracy. The importance and influence of "underlying conditions"—the characteristics of the nation-state—vary erratically from case to case; there are no set stages in the transition to democracy, and—most problematic—there is no assurance that the pot at the end of the rainbow is, in fact, a democracy in any recognizable form. There is not only the chance of a circuitous return to authoritarianism, though perhaps disguised as something more appealing, but also the possibility of innumerable permutations of democracy, or simply of democracies that perform so poorly or are so reckless that their admittance into the pantheon can only be grudgingly granted.

The embarrassing inability to foresee recent sweeping political sea changes, including prominently the demise of the Soviet Union, as well as the crumbling of authoritarian regimes throughout Latin America, has led to a call by some scholars for an intellectual retreat. Many scholars of politics have, in fact, retreated to "mid-level" theorizing (more appealing than labeling it "small-level") to avoid what has been called "the problem of indeterminacy" (more appealing than calling it "being wrong").

Narrow political questions are explored, sometimes with quantitative analysis and formal modeling. Increasingly, praise is reserved for those who can isolate independent variables and express their explanatory weight in the most parsimonious analysis, even if what is explained is only a hypothetical case with stringent assumptions or a very small piece of a complex political puzzle. Adhering to this fashionable methodology, in turn, reinforces intellectual pointillism since unwieldy political puzzles overwhelm or just bog down in scientific methodologies.

Scholars who engage in Herculean efforts to prove with temerity a relationship between two or more specific political variables must believe that the ultimate usefulness of their work will be in constructing an accurate "big picture" of politics. However, efforts at synthesis cannot wait until "everything has been learned." Instead, continuous, constant exercises are needed, incomplete but helpful efforts to understand the world. An ontological-epistemological reorientation is necessary, superseding the study of uniformity and the search for universal political patterns. All too often, scholarship on important topics at the level of the nation-state leads to the unique—so there can be no discovery of replicable behavior or outcomes. Efforts at generating theories—laws—about politics are misdirected and, given the record to date, likely to be futile, too.

The self-congratulatory pursuit of theory should be recast as a humble quest for better understanding of society. Whatever contributes to such understanding is welcome, including empirical detail, the untangling of complexity, the tracing of political processes, and the identification and measurements of relationships and probabilities. Description deserves to be rehabilitated. Different areas of the world—specific places and the people who inhabit them—warrant as much interest as the abstract processes of politics in which the conduct of politics is stripped of its context. In the end, the purpose of scholarship is to better understand the world, with all its richness and diversity.

In setting out to explore analytically a corner of the world, such as the countries of Central America, there is thus not much in the way of conceptual guidance or even encouragement. There seemingly is not much more to frame examination than the basic definitions that exist for the political entities of the region: country, nation, government, and state. And even with such a modest beginning, it is best to proceed with patience and caution.

The word "country" is loosely used. It is defined as the territory of a nation. What is a nation? A nation is a large number of people of mainly common descent, language, and history usually inhabiting a territory bounded by defined limits and forming a society under one government. What is government? Government is a form of organization of the state. What is the state? The state is the organized political community of a nation. Such definitions are circular and so imprecise. Thus, not surprisingly, the terms are used interchangeably, especially country and the combination nation-state. Still, these concepts, when disaggregated, can help an inquiry into the tack of a particular geographic region.

There are some more extensive definitions—and thoughtful discussions—of nation and state. The early-twentieth-century German sociologist Max Weber, who continues to cast a long intellectual shadow, defined the state as an organization that successfully claims and upholds a monopoly on the legitimate use of physical force within a given territory. Through its right to use force, the state permits some to prevail over others, but dominance is only achieved through successful competition to gain control over the seats and instruments of authority. Weber identified three legitimate routes to power: traditional domination by the patriarch or prince; charismatic domination by the prophet, warlord, or party leader; and legal domination by the bureaucrat or state servant. Of these three ideal types, Weber preferred legal domination, with its "routinization," order, harmony, and efficiency in the bureaucratic organization of the state.

A more contemporary definition of the state by a colleague at Harvard University, Merilee Grindle, provides a reassuring continuity. She sees the state as a set of ongoing institutions for social

control and authoritative decision-making and implementation. The state, she asserts, desires to establish and maintain internal and external security, to generate revenue, and to achieve hegemony over alternative forms of social organization. The state's abilities, she cautions, however, are influenced by economic conditions and degrees of social mobilization as well as by the legitimacy and internal cohesion of the state itself. Grindle's definition draws attention to what many find notable about states in Latin America: their combination of power and fragility. States may exercise considerable power; however, competition for authority can sap and subvert the state. Moreover, the power to control does not equate with the ability to transform, to develop the economy, or even to provide valued social services. States are often Janus-faced: simultaneously strong and weak.

Nations are counted and disaggregated with a census. Their attitudes, values, and propensities are gauged with surveys. However, a nation's true complexity—the richness of its culture—is unraveled only with painstakingly slow observation and analysis. Reaching conclusions is tricky; cultural differences are difficult to identify and measure with any precision. Leonard Binder, in an expansive essay published decades ago, suggested what should be obvious but which nonetheless is still often overlooked: culture is neither monolithic nor homogeneous. Nor is it static. Binder added, in a beguiling way, that in any culture—or nation—there are "great traditions" and "little traditions." What might these be? Which kind of tradition weighs more in explaining the tack countries take? A colleague of Binder, Lucian Pye, wrote evocatively of the pressures induced by change, and in particular of the stress on national identity stemming from foreign influences. This issue is enduring, and it has to be especially important in small, poor countries like those of Central America.

"State" and "nation," thus, are heady terms that require care when being used to portray specific countries. Moreover, putting the terms together, linking them with a hyphen, entails a further complexity: unraveling the relationship of one to the other. In all countries, political, economic, and social change is mediated by both national identity and the rules and norms of state institutions. National identity is not exogenous to state institutions; state institutions, in turn, are not exogenous to national identity. There is an obscure but symbiotic relationship between national identity and the state. Put differently, baldly perhaps, politics is forcefully shaped by the living legacy of history. There are always choices to be made in politics, to be sure, just as there are accidents, the diffusion of ideas, intrusions from abroad, and other ways in which politics is rendered unpredictable. But the context of national politics is important, weighty, and frequently less malleable than might be desired.

Countries are replete with values, habits, customs, symbols, traditions, institutions, rituals, ceremony, and myth. They are embedded in the nation and they are embedded in the state. And the nation and the state are jointly set in a corner of the world, in a specific territory, one having a unique endowment. Political identity begins with geography. The enigma of countries lies in their peculiarities and in the ways in which these thousand peculiarities—the accumulation of idiosyncratic endowments and histories—shape the conduct of politics.

Regime changes are rare but consequential. And so they attract attention. But the changing of regimes is not done in a vacuum. Regime changes take place only in specific countries, and so these changes—such as the turn to democracy and unfettered markets—are grafted onto an intricate web of deep, knobby, and dark roots.

The approach taken here is in part to highlight the many forces that shape political and economic outcomes, but also in part to illuminate these same outcomes—shining focused light most prominently on regime type and performance. It is widely recognized that there are many confounding variables which influence the course of a country. Less appreciated are the many varieties of outcomes for countries. In the lexicon of science, there are not only many independent variables, but there is also no grand dependent variables, comparable across cases. Terms bandied about to describe countries, such as "liberalism," "democracy," and "market economy," frequently obscure and confuse more than they clarify. In studying polities, it is best to neither start nor end with labels.

Liberalism is especially problematic as an analytical category. In Central America, liberalism has had widely divergent meanings and political import over the course of the region's history. In the aftermath of the American and French Revolutions, it was associated with freedom from monarchy—and from the Spanish monarchy in particular—and it favored self-government as a protection against tyranny. In the aftermath of independence, especially in the late nineteenth and early twentieth centuries, liberalism was associated with a drive for economic modernization, and it was employed to batter away at the privileges of the church and at other impediments to the expansion of private property and investments in export-generating activities. For much of the twentieth century, the most conspicuous vestige of liberalism was the political party of the Nicaraguan dynasty of the Somozas, incongruously known as the Liberal Party. During their long tenure, liberalism stood for personal liberties and anti-communism.

Liberalism all but disappeared from the political lexicon of the region during the turmoil of the 1970s and 1980s, but it reemerged with force—and with apparent unanimity—after the conflicts ended. In its latest gestation, it is equated with democracy and unfettered markets. Political discourse—rhetoric—and even constitutions, government organization, and public policies can all be misleading. Yes, ideas and ideologies matter. But history gives birth to stubborn political styles capable of transforming—bending and refracting—ideas that are either contagious or convenient for political elites to embrace. Democracy and unfettered markets can be molded into many different outcomes, some strikingly different from others. Such is the case today in Central America.

GEOGRAPHY AND MYTH

Over a tea in Princeton in the spring of 1942, the mathematician Paul Erdos introduced Peter Lax to Albert Einstein, saying he was a talented young Hungarian mathematician. Einstein turned to Erdos and asked, "Why mention Hungarian?"

Central Americans, on the other hand—and, indeed, all Latin Americans—readily identify themselves on the basis of their nationality. As a colleague at INCAE says, "Only poets and politicians speak of Latin America; all others in the region identify themselves on the basis of their nationality." Salvadorans who migrate to the United States because they feel they have no opportunity—no hope—in El Salvador, nonetheless continue to identify themselves as Salvadorans and commonly feel distinct from other migrants who, despite sharing many characteristics, such as race, class, language, religion, are from other countries, including, even, neighboring Guatemala, Honduras, and Nicaragua. Guatemalans, in turn, are no different in preferring the company of their own kind, and neither are Hondurans, Nicaraguans, or Costa Ricans. The countries of Central America are poor, each with a treacherous social landscape, but they all have the benefit of having a nation: a population that, in the words of the scholar Benedict Anderson, is a political community, imagined as both inherently limited and sovereign. In each of the five countries of the isthmus, this imagined political community is all-inclusive and strikingly coterminous with the territory of each country. Borders define not just the reach of states, but also of nations.

The countries of Europe, or at least of Western Europe, are judged to have a close match between nation and state, but one that was slow in coming, the result of the tribulations of hundreds of years. Elsewhere, though, especially in the many countries created haphazardly by European colonists, the confluence of nation and state is often missing, exacerbating the difficulties of government and economic development. When populations first and foremost define themselves by race, religion, caste, tribe, or maternal language, governing a country is a true challenge.

The five Central American countries, though, have constructed nations, despite the absence of any unique racial or ethnic "stock." Indeed, nations have been built on the horror of the "encounter" between the indigenous peoples of the isthmus and Spanish *conquistadores,* and they have had to accommodate the crippling class and racial divisions of colonialism. The construction of nations in Central America has been dependent on overcoming—or forgetting—the "birth" of the nations. In this region, there are no prophets, no Founding Fathers, certainly not, anyway, of the nations.

What is important, though, in the construction of nations is not actual history, but collective memory and how it is shaped socially, even politically. Myths and traditions that define and uphold national identity are invented. Political interests, veiled or masked as they may be, are partly behind the invention of national identity. Elites find "the social glue" of nationalism appealing, even useful. However, nationalism also appears, at least in Central America, to emerge partly out of the experience of living together in a particular setting, with unique endowments of geography, local cultural quirks, shared fears (including, prominently, of neighbors), and other idiosyncratic factors. Geography and myth are intertwined in the formation of nations. The construction of states seems more deliberate, more of a political project, but accidents of geography surely matter here, too.

Nation and state matter because they shape opportunities and fortunes. For example, those residing in Rivas, in the south of Nicaragua, are not really any different from those residing nearby in Liberia, in the north of Costa Rica. Residents of the two cities share race, religion, language, culture, and just about everything else except nation and state—that is, citizenship. This difference, though, matters so much because, as one Nicaraguan bluntly put it, "One country works, and the other doesn't." Central Americans are, to a large extent, hostage to the region's nations and states.

The issue is much broader, too, than just the comparative "performance" of individual countries: whether a country is a "winner" or a "loser." Considerable social and political capital is invested in "the nation" and "the state," "the country." There are opportunity costs: these resources could be invested elsewhere, in other kinds of social projects, in other kinds of social organization. Nationalism is distracting, masking regional, class, racial, and gender divisions. Maybe it obscures poverty and backwardness, too.

The arbitrary division of the isthmus into five nations also has implications for the integration of the region into the world economy. Are the small nation-states, with their roots in the Spanish colonialism of the sixteenth, seventeenth, and eighteenth centuries, appropriate—best suited—for participating in the ferocious world markets of the twenty-first century? Probably not. Nation-states—countries—are arbitrary, capricious, and illusionary divisions, built as much on myths and self-serving social memories as on geography and political decisions. However, countries matter: they profoundly shape perceptions of social identity and, more importantly, welfare. In a region that has always been poor and where so many live in poverty, economic performance is critical. The dice have been entrusted to nation-states and their governors.

Interpreting the history of Central America, untangling the web of facts and figures, deciding what is important, what is revealing, is a daunting task. Nearly all of the renowned *conquistadores* passed through Central America: including, among others, Cristóbal Colón, Vasco Núñez de Balboa, Francisco Pizarro, Diego de Almargo, Sebastián de Benalcázar, Pedro Arias de Avila (Pedrarias), Hernán Cortés, Cristóbal de Olid, Pedro de Alvarado, Gil González Dávila, and Francisco Hernández de

Córdoba. They came via Santo Domingo, Panama City, or Mexico, but always with the same intention: searching for a passage by which fleets of ships could continue sailing east to Asia, to the "spice islands." There was competition to see who would find the passage first and so exercise control over the navigation between the Atlantic and the Pacific Oceans. Geography attracted the Spanish.

Once it was clear that in Central America there was no passage between the two oceans, and likewise no great civilization to plunder, most of the Spanish departed. The few who stayed took from Indians what gold there was to be had, enslaved Indians for sale elsewhere, and, in time, employed Indian labor for mining (silver, in what is now Honduras), raising mules (for Panama's inter-oceanic traffic), or logging (for ship building). The Spanish were brutal. The Spanish priest Bartolomé de las Casas recounts in *The Devastation of the Indies:*

> In the year one thousand five hundred and twenty-three, at the end of the year, this same tyrant [Pedrarias] went into Nicaragua to subjugate that most flourishing province and a sorrowful hour it was when he entered that land. Who could exaggerate the felicity, the good health, the amenities of that prosperous and numerous population? Verily it was a joy to behold that admirable province with its big towns, some of them extending three or four leagues, full of gardens and orchards and prosperous people. But because this land is a great plain without any mountains where the people could take refuge, they had to suffer cruel persecutions. . . . He once sent fifty horsemen with pikes. . . . Not a single human being survived that massacre. . . . The greatest and most horrible pestilence that has laid waste the province of Nicaragua was the freedom given by the Governor to his subordinates in the matter of petitioning slaves from the caciques [native rulers]. . . . The Governor could obtain fifty slaves

> at a time by threatening the caciques with being burned at the stake or thrown to the fierce dogs if they refused. . . . For this transaction was aided by six or seven ships voyaging along the coast to take on board and sell the surplus requisitioned slaves in Panama and Peru. And all those captives soon died.

Ironically, in the early colonial history of Central America, the indigenous population—not land—was coveted.

The first Spanish settlements in the isthmus were urban, located in part by favorable geography and in part by the proximity of Indians, who nonetheless had to be resettled, moved from dispersed settlements into towns, where they provided labor and tribute. The region was poor and a backwater of the Spanish empire. There was no great source of wealth, but what wealth existed depended upon Indian labor. Indeed, the first "border" dispute in the region was between the Spaniards of Pedrarias (settled in what is now Nicaragua) and the Spaniards of Pedro de Alvarado (settled in what is now El Salvador). What was disputed was "ownership" of the Indians living along the banks of the Lempa River. Both parties asked the Spanish Crown for clear borders (*límites bien señalados*), but the Crown appears to have made land grants to *conquistadores* with a deliberate margin of uncertainty to keep the *conquistadores* quarreling among themselves and dependent on the Crown to mediate.

The most serious conflict, though, between the early Spanish settlers and the Crown was over the inheritance of Indians. Settlers contended that the Crown had granted unconditional ownership of the Indians to Spanish *conquistadores,* giving their descendants the right of inheritance. The Crown never agreed; asserting that upon the death of the Spaniards, the Indians returned to the "ownership" of the Crown. The Crown worried that if there were no Indians, there would be no Spaniards. Colonization would halt. However, with the absence of the ability to transfer control of Indians to heirs, there was no incentive for Spanish settlers to husband Indians. They were treated brutally—exploited without mercy.

The Catholic Church, with its many attendant religious orders, was a presence in colonial Central America, often more so than the scarce representatives of the Spanish Crown. The Church was caught in a dilemma. The proselytizing of Indians was facilitated by their resettlement in urban communities, but resettlement also made the Indians easier prey. The Church accepted tribute, too, but it clashed with the rapacity of Spanish settlers. It is telling that during the middle of the sixteenth century, a bishop in León, Nicaragua, was assassinated by enraged Spanish settlers.

The Catholic Church provided an incipient sense of community, one that was hierarchical but nonetheless inclusive. The Christian year was marked by numerous processions, which were social gatherings. Everyone participated. Spaniards marched first, followed by mestizos, and, in the rear, Indians. Likewise, all were welcome in church. Spaniards sat in the front. Behind them sat mestizos. Indians sat in the back. (A Nicaraguan from an upper-class family remembers his mother telling him as a boy, "Even in heaven there is hierarchy: God, seraphim, cherubim, archangels, and angels.")

The Catholic Church also joined the Crown and its representatives in providing a "worldview," one that included a distrust—or even hatred—of "others": Lutherans, Calvinists, and later, French liberals. Conversely, the Catholic Church furthered the embracing of the Spanish language and the social customs of Spain.

Initially, the bureaucratic center of the Spanish presence in Central America was in what is now Honduras. But Bishop Francisco Marroquín persuaded the Crown to move its offices to the highlands of Guatemala. The authority of the Crown was recognized in the immediate vicinity of its offices. Thus, when the Crown decreed that Spaniards and Africans could not reside in Indian communities because, as a colonial official said, Spanish and African men are like "wolves among sheep" with Indian women, the ruling was observed in the Guatemalan highlands. But elsewhere, where the administrative reach of the Crown was weak, there was little compliance. Today, as a result, Guatemala still has an indigenous population in the highlands, whereas elsewhere in the isthmus, mestizos predominate. (The mountains of the highlands, which made travel difficult during the colonial era, surely also helped protect the Indian communities.)

Political organization stabilized during the second half of the sixteenth century. The Audiencia, a tribunal established in Guatemala in 1548, acquired by 1570 jurisdiction over the entire region, from Chiapas to Costa Rica. It was the "Kingdom of Guatemala." The president of the Audiencia also fulfilled the functions of Captain General and Governor. Nominally subordinate to the Crown's representatives in Mexico, in reality Guatemala's fledgling bureaucracy continued to communicate directly with Madrid, where all decisions of any importance were made and where all officials were appointed. In the larger scheme of the Spanish empire, though, Central America was insignificant and all but forgotten. Years could pass without the arrival of any ships from Spain.

The Kingdom of Guatemala was a mosaic of administrative units, governing bodies, and magistrates. Settlements concentrated in the central highlands and on the Pacific slopes. Here the climate was more agreeable and Indians more numerous and more easily subjugated. The dense tropical forests of the Atlantic slopes remained a difficult frontier. Spanish control was limited to a narrow costal strip around the Port of Trujillo in Honduras, around the mouth of the San Juan River in Nicaragua, and a small stretch of the Atlantic Coast in Costa Rica. Pirates were a menace. In 1641, a Portuguese ship carrying slaves from Guinea broke up off the coast of Honduras, and the Africans ended up, according to the reports of the Spanish authorities, mixing with "infidel Indians," the Mosquitos of Honduras and Nicaragua. The *zambos-mosquitos,* egged on by English interlopers, attacked Spanish settlements including the Guatemalan city of Flores. But more than anything, they probably served as a cover for English logging and trade along the coast, which reached such proportions that eastern Guatemala became "British Honduras" (which, despite objections from Guatemala, attained its independence in 1980, under the name Belize). Similarly, eastern

Nicaragua became an "English protectorate" (though it was incorporated "back into" Nicaragua in 1894).

By the beginning of the seventeenth century, the Indian population of the isthmus had declined such that many Spanish settlers and their descendants were forced to take economic refugee in ranches (*haciendas*), dedicating themselves to little more than subsistence agriculture. Notwithstanding brief upswings from the exports of indigo, cocoa, and silver, the region became progressively stagnant. There were afflictions, too: plagues, epidemics, failed harvests, earthquakes, and other natural disasters. Spain provided no assistance, not even a defense of intrusions from the Atlantic coast.

On the eve of independence there was a sense—at least among the creoles (those of Spanish descent born in the Americas)—of what it meant to be Guatemalan, from Guatemala City and its environs, and what it meant to be from the "provinces," from El Salvador, Honduras, Nicaragua, and Costa Rica. Those from Guatemala felt superior given that they held the seat of government, had closer ties to Spain, and had received from the crown the splendid title "Very Loyal and very Noble." Plus, Guatemalans had a university (the third oldest in the Americas), an archbishop with a grand cathedral (*catedral metropolitana*), and the only commercial guild in the region. For their part, Salvadorans, Hondurans, and Nicaraguans resented the privileges of Guatemala. Inhabitants of Costa Rica, the most distant "province" and the last to be settled, resented Guatemala's authority, too, and preferred to trade—illegally—with the English based in Jamaica. The first "national identities" in Central America were tied to sentiments of either superiority or resentment toward neighbors. What all shared, though, was a sense of insignificance and passivity. Decisions were made elsewhere.

The independence of Central America came unwittingly in 1821 with the independence of Mexico from Spain. Initially, the isthmus was to be bound to Mexico, but annexation was short-lived (though Chiapas separated from Guatemala and united with Mexico). There was an attempt at building a union of Central American states, with the establishment in 1824 of the Federation of Central America, linking Guatemala, El Salvador, Honduras, Nicaragua, and Costa Rica. But communication was difficult among the states. There was an imbalance of the population, too. In 1824, the population of the isthmus was perhaps just over a million, but nearly half of it was concentrated in Guatemala. In the hinterland, there were the long-standing resentments of Guatemala's strength. Guatemalans, in turn, were convinced that the "provincials" were envious of their grandeur and the "magnificence" of their buildings. The Federal Republic had a brief and unsettled existence, disintegrating in 1838.

The five states became independent but had to wrestle with their own internal rivalries, such as between Comayagua and Tegucigalpa in Honduras and between León and Granada in Nicaragua. There were also ideological divisions, between liberals—eager to innovate, to modernize—and conservatives, clinging to the colonial way of life. The clarity of visions for governing was clouded by personal ambitions and rivalries. The world outside intruded, too, offering new political alliances and suggesting novel forms of participating in the world economy.

Coffee was introduced into Costa Rica, and production expanded rapidly, spreading elsewhere in the isthmus and bringing with it many social changes. The discovery of gold in California in 1848 led to many travelers from the east coast of the United States to California trampling through Nicaragua and Panama. In 1855, an adventurer from Tennessee named William Walker and a small army of mercenaries set up a phantom government in Nicaragua, with the hope of annexing the country to the United States. The spooked Central American countries united and defeated him with a multinational army. Negotiations at the turn of the twentieth century between the United States and Nicaragua over the construction of a canal linking the Atlantic and Pacific Oceans failed, with the canal ultimately being built in Panama (long part of Colombia), but the region's strategic importance was nonetheless underscored, as was its proximity to the muscular United States.

State formation, though, seems to have been driven in great part by the triumph of liberalism in the 1870s, leading to an

uninterrupted effort at modernizing countries with the guidance—or at least tacit support—of government. Church lands were, in one way or another, transferred to private entrepreneurs. Labor was cajoled into meeting the needs of export-driven agriculture. Roads and railroads were built, telegraph lines were laid, and ports were modernized. State-led efforts at modernization did not challenge colonial divisions of race and class; indeed, they may well have accentuated them. Moreover, the philosophy of liberalism, despite its influence on the management of the economy, made little dent on the style of governing. Still, governments, in staffing bureaucracies, recruiting and training armies, building roads and railways, and, in time, building schools with civic classes, helped to cement a nascent nationalism, a personal identification with the respective countries. Even such pedestrian endeavors as the coining of money and the printing of stamps, both replete with "national" symbols, were a help. Sometime in the middle of the twentieth century, it came to be—everywhere in the isthmus—that when a bugle announced at the end of the day the lowering of the national flag, drivers would stop their cars and join pedestrians in placing their right hands on their hearts, showing their devotion to their country.

The production of bananas by United States companies probably, ultimately, helped integrate the countries of the region, especially Honduras, "the most Atlantic" (and so Caribbean) of the countries of the isthmus. Though shipments of bananas from the coast of Honduras were sold in New Orleans as early as the 1870s, it was at the beginning of the twentieth century that United States companies developed a real toe-hold in the region, with considerable land concessions. The Atlantic costal regions of Guatemala, Honduras, and Costa Rica were remade. Salaried laborers came from Jamaica to work on the large, foreign-owned plantations. These African American immigrants mixed with the few inhabitants of the same origin who had lived on the coast since the seventeenth century, and together they strengthened their Caribbean cultural traits, thereby separating even further this "other" Central America from that of the central highlands and the Pacific Coast. However, with time the sovereignty of the banana companies posed a political challenge that had to be confronted—and was successfully confronted—furthering the political (if not cultural) integration of individual countries.

Throughout the twentieth century there were serious—violent—conflicts in the Central American countries. But it is notable that none of these conflicts led to a questioning of the existence of either the nations or the states of the isthmus. El Salvador, for example, was wracked by violence in the 1930s and again in the 1970s and 1980s. But none of the parties to the strife ever questioned that there was—and should be—an El Salvador populated by Salvadorans. When in 1969 war broke out between El Salvador and Honduras, rifts within El Salvador quickly receded. Centuries have not erased the racial and class divisions in Central America created by the "encounter," but the nation-states that have been built in the isthmus are inviolable. There are, to be sure, pockets of "non-believers," in the highlands of Guatemala and in stretches of the Atlantic coast, but, recognizing the immutability of nation and state, they acquiesce.

All the central facets of the countries of Central America can be found in the region's history, and the keys to the ways in which the five countries differ from one another can surely be found, too, by digging more deeply into history, in particular to regional history. However, it is an open question just how much the present—the living—nationalism and acceptance of the state in the region comes from an understanding of history, even of the truncated and edited history that comprises what is called "social memory." The population of the region is young: the average age is sixteen. The level of education is poor. Moreover, poverty, climate, and natural disasters have conspired to leave few documents, paintings, monuments, public buildings, or other material—and visual—links to the region's past.

Interest in history is limited, surely in large part because of the exigencies of daily life. A Costa Rican in his early thirties was revealing when he said, looking back on his education: "From what I remember, we went directly from Cristóbal Colón to independence. And I don't remember much said either about the period from independence until today."

For the great majority of Central Americans, national identity is seemingly just a given, reinforced by the immediacy of geographical reference points—whether plazas and churches or volcanoes and lakes—and prosaic cultural practices. All that is local is familiar and so comfortable, from newspapers and radio stations, to brands of consumer goods, to popular expressions, slang and accents, to food. There is also the collective experience of living through reigns of government (riled as they may be), sensational crimes, natural disasters, and other dramas of life. Finally, there is soccer—and soccer rivalries.

The soccer rivalries are local: with other Central American countries. Central Americans commonly believe that each country is different from one another, and this difference is ascribed to the "nation"—the people, each judged to have a different temperament, with one or more flaws. Central Americans have nicknames for each other and a quirky set of stereotypes that are voiced in private conversations or in large public gatherings where anonymity is guaranteed (such as screaming at soccer matches). Still read is a pair of articles about the difference between Nicaraguans (*nicas*) and Costa Ricans (*ticos*) published in the May 1964 issue of *Revista Conservadora*: "El 'nica' y el 'tico', según un 'nica'" and "El 'tico' y el 'nica', según un 'tico'" (Nicaraguans and Costa Ricans, according to a Nicaraguan, and Costa Ricans and Nicaraguans, according to a Costa Rican). Similar articles could be written about other paired comparisons, such as between Guatemalans and Salvadorans. These perceptions of differences between "us" and "them" may just be myths, but they are part of what defines countries.

Nations and states may have their roots in geography and carefully constructed and nurtured myths, but their sustenance—at least in Central America—seems more prosaic. Indeed, ironies abound. The celebrated coffee of Honduras is the brand El Indio, which dates back to 1933. However, the coffee is marketed with the picture of a Sioux Indian, replete with an eagle feather headdress. (When asked about the misplaced image, a well-educated Honduran laughed and explained, "That was just taken from Hollywood.") Likewise, Salvadorans traveling to visit relatives in the United States commonly board their flights carrying boxes of fried chicken from El Campero, a Guatemalan-owned "fast-food" franchise inspired by the United States franchise Kentucky Fried Chicken (KFC). These ironies do not detract from the dignity of the pride in national identity. What they do suggest, though, is the malleability of nationalism, the ability to remake even what is foreign as one's own. This malleability of nationalism suggests its tenacity, its likely permanence. Inescapably it seems, the fate of Central Americans is tied to the fortunes of their small countries in the whirlwinds of the world.

LIBERALISM AND
DEMOCRACY

As a cluster of countries, Guatemala, El Salvador, Honduras, Nicaragua, and Costa Rica share, in addition to a geographical corner and a cultural affinity, a commitment to rule by liberalism. The locus of decision making may always be the nation-state, but at times powerful currents or forces lead political actors in different nations to make similar choices within a relatively compressed period of time. One such moment occurred in the 1980s, a period of sweeping change in Latin America. At the beginning of the decade, the majority of countries in the region were governed by authoritarian—military—regimes that pursued state-led economic development. However, by the first few years of the 1990s, every country in the region except for Cuba had a constitutional government and leaders elected in free and competitive elections. This abrupt embrace of democracy was remarkable. Moreover, a second major shift took place in the 1980s and early 1990s: the pursuit of market-based economic growth. Even in Cuba, where the country's leadership pledged continued allegiance to communism, economic policy was altered to give freer rein to markets.

The five Central American countries, which suffered from so much political turmoil in the 1980s, were surely washed by the same mystical, amorphous wave of democracy and economic reform that swept over the countries of South America and Mexico to the north. Nonetheless, Central America is under civilian—and market—rule for distinct reasons. Costa Rica has been an unwavering liberal democracy since 1948. In the four other countries of the isthmus, the path to democracy differed from the negotiated transitions in South America (and the snail-paced reforms in Mexico). It was fear of revolution in Guatemala, El Salvador, and Honduras and fear of counter-revolution in Nicaragua that led to the impetuous construction of liberal democracies. In all four countries, the United States played a deciding, though hardly unilateral, role. It could be said, crudely perhaps, that "imperialist intimidation" solved "the problem of soldiers and politics."

Central America's unlikely—and rushed—route to liberal democracy may not have been perceived as leading to durable regimes. However, democracy has been resilient and even stable in the isthmus. Municipal, congressional, and presidential elections have become sacrosanct. No other route to political power is sanctioned. Elections are free and competitive, and the results are respected: those who win govern. Central Americans vote at rates equal to or exceeding those of wealthy countries such as Japan, the United States, the United Kingdom, and France. Moreover, voters in the five Central American countries have consistently exercised caution at the polls, shunning political extremes and contributing themselves to the sobriety of elections. For example, in El Salvador's 2004 presidential election, the Farabundo Martí National Liberation Front lost, giving the more moderate National Republican Alliance an almost unheard-of (for Latin America) four successive terms of office. On the other side of the political spectrum, Guatemalans strongly rejected the ultra-conservative candidacy (scarcely hidden behind populist rhetoric) of former military ruler Efraín Ríos Montt in the 2003 presidential election. The Sandinista Daniel Ortega did win the 2006 presidential election in Nicaragua, but he won by replacing his former revolutionary rhetoric with a campaign of "peace, love, and unity" (and he won with less than half of the vote—the opposition was divided). Voting behavior in the five countries of the isthmus suggests the population at large has an overwhelming desire for political moderation.

Democracy has been sapped by weak institutions, the manipulation of political office by elected officials, a beleaguered and

under-funded public administration, and an awkward fit with liberalism. However, democracy has brought one monumental advance, one that overshadows all of its shortcomings—peace. Tens of thousands of Central Americans, above all Guatemalans, Salvadorans, and Nicaraguans, met with horrible deaths in the conflicts of the late 1970s and the 1980s. Violation of basic rights, of simple decency, was common. The myriad costs of the conflicts are beyond compare. Democracy purchased peace, or vice versa.

Dating the transition to democracy in Guatemala, El Salvador, and Honduras is difficult and perhaps not important. In all three countries, there was a concurrent, though not always neat, process of soldiers returning to the barracks and the holding of elections. There were meaningful elections in Guatemala and El Salvador during the 1980s, even before the ending of armed conflict and the signing of peace accords (in 1992 in El Salvador and 1996 in Guatemala). The transition to democracy in Nicaragua is commonly dated to the elections of 1990, which effectively marked the end of the Sandinista Revolution—and the counter-revolution. In all four countries, there have been numerous elections since the turbulent 1980s, and furthermore, the prerogatives of the military have diminished. In Guatemala, El Salvador, Honduras, and Nicaragua, the military not only is constitutionally bound, but also now absorbs less than 1 percent of gross national product (GNP).

Just how democracy is understood—as a political theory and as a kind of government—in Central America is open to interpretation. Liberalism and democracy are often conflated. Liberalism is best understood as constitutional and limited government, the rule of law, and the protection of individual rights. Democracy, in contrast, is understood as the selection of governing authorities by universal suffrage in free, competitive elections. The initial priority in Central America—as in all of Latin America—was the holding of elections. It is surely easier to hold genuinely free elections than to fulfill liberalism's commitment to the rule of law. But Central American countries have attempted to be "liberal democracies," fulfilling the aspirations of both liberalism (rule by law and respect of human rights) and democracy (with its insistence on the election of rulers). As elsewhere, liberal ideals and democratic procedures have become interwoven.

An ambitious study of the political culture of young people in Central America, based on surveys of high school students in all five countries of the isthmus, gives a sense of how democracy is understood in the region. In El Salvador, for example, students were asked what they thought were the principal characteristics of democracy. The answers: satisfaction of economic necessities, 34 percent; respect for minorities, 20 percent; opportunity to vote, 18 percent; liberty to criticize and protest, 14 percent; the existence of numerous political parties, 5 percent, and "don't know" (*no sabe*), 10 percent. It is curious that the most frequent attribute of democracy is judged to be the "satisfaction of economic necessities"; perhaps respondents offered what they thought should be the principal gift of democracy. Otherwise, though, the responses suggest an expectation for not just democracy, but for liberal democracy.

For those who never made it to high school—or who never will—the understanding of democracy may be vague. There may only be a sense of power wielded from afar by "others," a sense of entitlement, or a frustration at not receiving more "help." The agreement of elites to hold elections was not accompanied by a broad campaign to educate citizens in the principles of democracy—they were just encouraged to vote. In Guatemala there may be, too, cultural barriers to understanding liberal democracy as a political model for governing the country. Presidential candidate Álvaro Colom elaborated in an interview published in 2000 in *The New Leader*:

> An estimated 60 percent of the population is indigenous. Indigenous groups do not speak of a "political system"; they speak of community consensus, and their conception of community is very local. . . . How do you have a functioning nation-state, one where indigenous groups participate actively in protecting their political interests, and yet still respect the cultural practices of other

indigenous groups for whom participation in Western political institutions is deemed undesirable?

Resolving this dilemma is a true challenge, and perhaps not even possible. Elsewhere in Central America, there is a reliance on an alchemy of a fragmentary understanding of democracy, patience, and apathy. An absence of an understanding of democracy, of how it works and what it can and cannot offer, surely retards participation in political parties—the intermediaries between voters and the government—and in interest groups. Without widespread and sober participation in political parties, it is easier for opportunistic individuals or groups "to capture" political parties and either to manipulate them for selfish gain or to otherwise engage in irresponsible behavior. It is notable, too, that many of the political parties in Central America predate the transition to democracy. Indeed, the Liberal Party of Honduras was founded in 1891; the other party in what is essentially a two-party system, the National Party, was founded in 1902. Electoral politics is fierce in Honduras, but both parties are widely believed to be beholden to elites and in fact are accused of collusion. It is quipped in Honduras that they "eat from the same plate." In Nicaragua, too, the dominant political parties all predate the country's transition to democracy—and all are held to be controlled by powerful, charismatic individuals. Nicaragua's former vice-president Sergio Ramírez, a celebrated novelist, has said that the central tension in Nicaragua has been and continues to be between institutions and individuals. This tension is most apparent in those organizations responsible for faithfully aggregating citizen interests and preferences—political parties.

The region's healthiest political parties are in El Salvador, where the ideological schism between the National Republican Alliance (ARENA) and the Farabundo Martí National Liberation Front (FMLN) thwarts collusion and instead propels the parties to be responsible. Yet, it is unclear why the same potential ideological schism in Nicaragua has not led to an adherence to principles and so to spirited competition. The most likely answer is simply "individuals," the leadership that firmly—and undemocratically—controls Nicaragua's two dominant political parties: the Liberal Constitutional Party (commonly just referred to as the Liberal Party) and the Sandinista National Liberation Front (FSLN). Guatemala's political parties have long been mercurial. The current dominant political parties came into existence in the aftermath of the country's transition to democracy. The National Advancement Party (PAN) was founded by professionals and business leaders in Guatemala City eager to emulate El Salvador's ARENA, judged to be a "modern" political party. The PAN is always being remade, but it—and the smaller, ad hoc parties that it spawns—occupy a prominent space in the center of Guatemala's political continuum. The Guatemalan Republican Front (FRG) is decidedly conservative, though with a populist streak. There is, too, an unstable coalition of groups on the left, able, at least, to field a common candidate in presidential elections. Costa Rica has long had two dominant political parties: the National Liberation Party (PLN) and the Social Christian Unity Party (PUSC). In all five countries there are other, small political parties trying to break the hegemony—and lethargy— of the larger, dominant political parties. But voters in Central America, as critical as they are of established parties, hesitate to embrace new political parties, many of which, too, seem beholden to charismatic (or not so charismatic) individuals.

A Mexican political analyst, José Woldenberg, has offered an amusing but insightful catalogue of fifty-two definitions of political parties. He says they are, among other things, points of ideological reference, networks of relationships and interests, generators of agendas, analyses, and solutions, but they are also, he claims, labyrinths, theaters of rhetoric, and coliseums for gladiators. Electoral campaigns in Central America are intense and serious, but also rife with vague promises and unsustainable proposals. These kinds of campaigns heighten expectations that can only, in time, be dashed. For example, in the 2003 presidential election in Guatemala, then-president Alfonso Portillo and the candidate of his party (the FRG), Efraín Ríos Montt, offered "financial compensation" to the former members of the government-organized militias who served as a paramilitary force during the counter-insurgency campaign of the 1980s. Shortly before the election, a partial payment was made to 497,000 Guatemalans. The opposition candidate, Óscar Berger, won the presidency and so inherited the sizeable financial commitment, which aggravated an already alarming government deficit. Coping with the commitment was all the more difficult since the FRG won the largest number of seats in congress.

Those elected to the presidency, like Berger, find it difficult to govern. The Central American regimes are presidential democracies (as distinct from parliamentary democracies). The president, elected independently, is a powerful figure, yet hemmed in by congress, the judiciary, a torpid bureaucracy, and more generally by poverty—everything is scarce. Moreover, there are many other political actors, ranging from business organizations to angry students to the United States embassy, with pressing claims. There are many demands and few resources with which to meet them.

The presidents of Central America are sometimes said to be "paper tigers": tigers because administration is so centralized, but only of paper because power is dispersed among so many political actors. Indeed, a former president of Guatemala, Álvaro Arzú, publicly lamented, "I have authority, not power." Similarly, the former president of Costa Rica, José María Figueres complained: "Managing congress is like guiding a clowder of black cats in the middle of the night, without light, without even a candle." The difficulty of working together, of finding common ground, is commonly explained by the kind of quip offered by a young official of the Liberal Party in Nicaragua: "Everyone is looking for their own bone." Despite campaign promises to the contrary, presidents cannot do much about such important problems as poverty, income inequality, and sluggish economic growth.

Indeed, a book was published in Guatemala with the title *Las promesas cumplidas por el presidente Alfonso Portillo* (The Promises Fulfilled by President Alfonso Portillo). The book has an attractive cover, listing Vinicio Montoya and Fausto Casasola as authors. But opening the book, the reader discovers there are only blank pages.

Still, presidents set the tone, and the agenda, for the government. Moreover, they have considerable discretion on issues that while not of sweeping import still offer advantages—or disadvantages—to specific groups. Public administration is not always "rule bound." A former Nicaraguan minister of industry, Norman Caldera, who served in the administration of Arnoldo Alemán, told the following anecdote when asked about the conduct of public administration:

> Everyone comes to my office saying the President said this or that. My answer is always the same: tell the President to put it in writing. The President knows I say this and he thinks it is an amusing response. But one day two very influential businessmen came to my office and told me that the President had granted them a monopoly on the sale of sugar in the country. Surprised, I immediately called the President, who told me: "They're crazy!" I asked the President if I could put him on "speaker phone." He said yes. On hearing his answer, a booming, "You're crazy!" the two men left my office silently, embarrassed, with their heads hung low.

The story is amusing, but it is also telling.

The discretion of presidents—and of other ranking public officials—has contributed to a continuing problem of corruption, one that antecedes the transition to democracy but still shows little sign of abating. The sums involved, for such small, poor countries, can be staggering. Corruption—and other kinds of crime—suggest that the most serious shortcoming in the pursuit of liberal democracy in Central America concerns the gap in the rule of law. To a certain extent (one that cannot be quantified), the weakness of law in the five countries of Central America is a reflection of the way in which naked power—be it

economic or political—has been able to skirt democracy's social leveling. There is, in fact, no equality before the law.

The weakness of law in Central America is also a reflection of the shortcomings of public administration, evident throughout the bureaucracies of the state. In the 1980s, Central America may have changed its "regime type," but the machinery of the state—the bureaucracy—was unaltered. There have been efforts to "modernize" the state, with special success in El Salvador, but in many instances government offices lag in efficiency and responsiveness to public need. The judiciary system, in particular, is widely perceived as needing improvement in all five countries, requiring both political insulation and administrative reform. A more participatory political culture is needed, too, one that expects and demands more accountability from political leaders—and all public employees—and holds them to higher ethical standards.

Still, the countries of Central America are governed. There is no chaos or anarchy. States are not in question. There is no communal violence; there is a remarkable symmetry between borders and nations in the region. Infrastructure is maintained; public services are uneven but generally provided. The military has receded from public life, leaving civilians in positions of power. Elections are routine and honest. Democracy compels political leaders to be at least somewhat responsive to sharply felt needs or demands, the more so when electoral competition is fierce. Universal adherence to the rule of law is elusive, but basic human rights are respected, as are personal liberties. The press is vigorous in all five countries, always investigating and reporting on political failings and so goading elites to improve their performance. The press, like the public, is critical of the region's governments but embraces democracy—or at least is leery of alternatives.

There is, however, an absence of ideas—of political debate—in Central America. It is a period of very modest and carefully circumscribed passions. A leader of one of Guatemala's political parties commented: "Here in our headquarters we don't even have a library, but look at the election propaganda we have to offer. Unfortunately, in our countries, politics—the candidates—are sold just like fruit juice. What is important is marketing." A Nicaraguan politician offers a similar view: "Political parties have become stripped of ideology. Debates in congress, as well as within political parties, don't have anything to do with the discussion of ideas, only with the negotiation of interests." Ideological contestation is absent, and so missing, too, are bold ideas for harnessing the state to address poverty, inequality, and other pressing problems.

Liberalism places a faith in individual initiative. The usually unspoken, and certainly poorly understood, aspiration in Central America is that individual effort in the economy will lead to the "development" and the "modernization" of the countries of the isthmus, reducing, in stride, poverty and inequality. The "private sector"—the amalgamation of laborers, managers, entrepreneurs, and the country's stock of firms and capital—is seen as the engine of change. The country's natural resources, its geographical location, its governance, the quality of its public services, can all assist—or hinder—its progress, but still, in this era less is expected from the state and much is expected from society, the nation. To be sure, the five democracies of Central America differ in many ways. Perhaps each Central American country can even be said to have its own political style, one that transcends administrations. However these political differences are conceptualized, they help define the opportunities of the private sector, and they shape the success of individual initiatives.

In earlier epochs the countries of Central America embraced liberalism, above all with respect to the management of the economy. Dictators may have governed, but they often shied away from employing the state to guide the economy. Indeed, with the exception of Costa Rica and of Nicaragua during its decade-long Revolution, the countries of Central America never followed with any conviction Mexico and the South American countries in embracing state-led economic development. However, the countries of the isthmus did close their economies with high tariffs (which provided a convenient source of revenue as well as protection for "infant industries"). What is novel about the present embracing of liberalism in Central America is that it is accompanied by an across-the-board opening to the world economy. This opening takes place at a time of unprecedented world trade in goods and services, movement of people, and diffusion of ideas, information, and technology.

The transition to democracy assisted the countries of Central America in ending the traumatic conflicts of the late 1970s and the 1980s. Elections, too, solved the problem of regime succession, long a source of difficulties in the isthmus. Also, with democracy the countries of the region became more outwardly similar to other countries with which they have cultural, political, and economic ties. Still, it is the flinging of themselves into international markets where the small countries of Central America are "placing their bets." Much, including the continuing integrity of their states and their nations, is at stake. Yet how the five countries of Central America fare depends, at least in part, on the choices they make. And these choices frequently are political decisions.

UNFETTERED MARKETS

O n the eve of the Nicaraguan Revolution, in 1979, the population of Central America was estimated to be 17.4 million. A quarter of a century later, in 2004, the population had doubled, to 35 million. The most pronounced change in the economy of the five Central American countries since the political turmoil of the 1980s is, in fact, just that the population has grown and thus so has economic activity. But there are other important changes. Economies are much more diverse. There is a greater and more complex integration into the world economy. There is, too, a new, previously unimagined source of income for the region: remittances from the many Central Americans who have left their countries but who send money "home." What is constant is that the region remains poor. There is wealth in the region, much of it novel, but per capita incomes remain low. Looking at average incomes masks an inequitable distribution of income: poverty is endemic in the region—many Central Americans live in misery.

Long-established views of the Central American economy, some tired and trite, need to be replaced with an understanding of the ways in which the region's economy has changed in the aftermath of the turmoil of the 1980s. Documenting and analyzing these changes is not easy because they have been so sudden and are still unfolding. Even more challenging is fathoming just what is the significance of these changes. The enduring presence of the poor is worrisome. Why has their misery not eased? What hope exists for them?

For decades, analyses of Central America's economies focused overwhelmingly on agrarian issues: control of land, the production of agricultural commodities for export, terms of trade, subsistence farming by poor peasants, the landless, and the seemingly inexplicable domination of agrarian economies by cities, the capital in particular. This emphasis was fitting. Economies were overwhelmingly dependent on the export of a handful of traditional commodities: bananas, coffee, cotton, sugar, and beef. The Nicaraguan Revolution had as its setting, for example, an economy in which 80 percent of foreign exchange earnings, so necessary for small states, were from agriculture. Likewise, 70 percent of the population earned its living from the land. Paradoxically, while the rural areas of Nicaragua were the source of wealth, the most severe poverty in the country was—and continues to be—in rural areas.

The Sandinistas aspired to fulfill the promises of the Nicaraguan Revolution with far-reaching agrarian policies: investments in huge state farms, controlling private farming, management of credit and prices, land reform, the formation of cooperatives, and the organization of rural workers. Perhaps, too, it was the problems—and contradictions—with these same agrarian policies that were the undoing of the Revolution. State farms lost enormous amounts of money; well-heeled private farmers subverted state policies, absorbing resources but producing little; and the rural poor did not like what they were offered. Rural workers had their wages frozen in a bid to reduce production costs, and beneficiaries of the agrarian reform resented the imposition of cooperatives, restrictions on the sale of land, and—above all—price controls on their harvests. The "social base" of the counterrevolution, funded by the United States government, was none other than the intended beneficiary—poor rural Nicaraguans.

The success of the Sandinista-led insurgency in Nicaragua emboldened guerrilla groups in El Salvador and Guatemala. Fighting spread throughout many parts of rural El Salvador, disrupting agricultural production. Many farms were either torched by guerrillas or outright occupied. Between 1979 and 1982 alone, the production of coffee, cotton, and sugar fell by 50 percent. The

United States government pushed the Salvadoran government under siege to undertake a land reform with the hope of winning the allegiance—or least political neutrality—of the rural poor. Even though the land reform was modest, it nonetheless further disrupted agricultural production. Investment fell. Fearful owners fled to the relative safety of San Salvador or left the country altogether. Guatemala had been beset by guerrilla activity since the early 1960s, but this activity mushroomed in the late 1970s, prominently by the Guerrilla Army of the Poor. As in Nicaragua and El Salvador, violence disrupted agricultural production and frightened entrepreneurs and investors.

The United States government, presided over by Ronald Reagan, provided generous assistance to the Nicaraguan counter-revolution and "counter-insurgency" aid to the government of El Salvador. (Guatemala washed its hands of assistance from the United States government, irritated at the insistence of at least a modicum of respect for "human rights.") The United States government, and international financial institutions where the United States government has a significant voice, concurrently began pushing for political and economic reforms throughout Central America. The recipe for ending political strife and economic stagnation: democracy and economic liberalization. Foreign assistance, desperately needed, was "conditioned" on reform, and there was considerable cajoling. But the message fell, too, on a receptive audience, one tired and fearful. Costa Rica was exempt from being hectored about the merits of democracy, but—like its northern neighbors—it was suddenly awash in suggestions for economic reform, for prying open the economy, for moving from "import substitution" to "export promotion."

In the 1980s and into the 1990s, all five Central American countries began efforts to transform their economies, moving from the protection of local industry (such as it was) through various kinds of subsidies and high tariffs to a push for the promotion of exports, especially of non-traditional goods. As a first step, efforts were made to stabilize the economies, offering the private sector "a level playing field." Stabilizing the economy meant more than anything reducing inflation. Inflation was to be controlled, in turn, by constraining fiscal deficits that inevitably were covered with an increase in the money supply. Many, though hardly all, subsidies and other market distortions were cast aside. An eclectic mix of state enterprises in Costa Rica and Nicaragua were sold, and there was the privatization of utilities in Guatemala and El Salvador. In Honduras there were concessions to the private sector, such as for the management of airports. Everywhere government ministries simplified the regulations governing exports and otherwise tried to stimulate foreign commerce. Non-governmental organizations were created, often with aid from the United States government, to strengthen the private sector and foment businesses that could lead to exports. The most significant change, though, was the unilateral lowering of tariffs, from an average of 90 percent in the early 1980s to an average of 10 percent at the end of the 1990s. Finally, foreign direct investment was encouraged and even facilitated by legislation offering, for example, tax exemptions and desired infrastructure.

Those in business in Central America are revealing with the name they have bestowed on this change of economic regime: "the opening" (la apertura). For the private sector, the new economic paradigm is most significant for the "opening" it has brought to the world economy, opportunities but also a frightful competition. Even though economic liberalism places the private sector as the "motor" of economic development, those in business say the "opening" was not their doing, that instead it was the work of opportunistic politicians casting about for something new to offer and, above all, international financial organizations. Those in business say that the opening of the national economies to commerce and investment was inevitable, given powerful international trends. The private sector does not always welcome competition, but there is a shared sentiment captured by a prominent Salvadoran businessman who quips, "First competition makes you sick, then it makes you better."

Macro-economic statistics are not always reliable, but they do suggest the direction and scope of the changes in the economies of Central America since the strife of the 1980s. According to the Economic Commission for Latin America and the

Caribbean (ECLAC), throughout the decade of the 1990s, the economies of the region, taken together, grew by an average of 4 percent a year, with positive growth of at least 2 percent every year. Exports grew by an even more robust figure, contributing to the sentiment that growth was at least in part export-driven. Moreover, exports have become increasingly diverse. In 1990, Central America's exports of goods, measured in dollar value, were 13 percent less than they were in 1980, reflecting the tension and disruptions of the decade. There was little change, too, in the composition of exports. In 1990, the region exported goods worth 4.25 billion dollars. Traditional exports (coffee, bananas, cotton, meat, and sugar) made up 56 percent of this amount. Non-traditional exports contributed 9 percent. The remaining 36 percent of exports were from "free trade zones"—assembly plants, called *maquilas,* overwhelmingly producing textiles.

Eleven years later, in 2001, the value of the region's exports had more than doubled, to 10.2 billion dollars. Moreover, the composition of exports had changed. Traditional exports represented only 22 percent of these exports; indeed, the dollar value of these traditional exports was less than in 1990. In contrast, there was a sevenfold increase in non-traditional exports; in 2001 they accounted for 26 percent of the total value of exports. Non-traditional exports embrace an eclectic range of goods, for example: ornamental plants, pineapples, sugar peas, fresh and dried herbs, shrimp, hardwood doors, plastic pipes, and small kitchen appliances. "Other exports"—the output of *maquilas*—climbed, too, contributing 52 percent of export earnings for the isthmus. Here, too, there was increased diversity, including: automobile parts, sports equipment, and computer chips. The export of computer chips is significant; the sprawling Intel plant in Costa Rica annually generates a billion dollars' worth of exports— almost a fifth of the country's total exports. In sum, although the primary product of the region's many *maquilas* remains textiles, there has been a welcome growth and diversity in this novel sector—and, more generally, in the export of "goods."

In addition, in the 1990s, Central America, and Costa Rica in particular, developed its tourism industry—what is sometimes awkwardly referred to as an export of a service. In any case, tourism mushroomed, much of it an "eco-tourism," with the natural beauty of the region—its volcanoes, rainforests, and beaches—drawing many visitors, prominently from North America and Europe. In 2001, a representative year, tourism generated 2.3 billion dollars in revenue for the region. Tourism is, in fact, the most important source of revenue for Costa Rica, which receives 23 percent of all visitors to the region but which captures 41 percent of the region's earnings from tourism (since visitors to the country stay longer and spend more). Even in Nicaragua, though, which has been slow to develop its infrastructure to support tourism, more is now earned from visitors than from the country's principal agricultural export—coffee.

Foreign direct investment in Central America—another source of dollars—has grown and is now considerable, with a peak in 1998 of 2.6 billion dollars. In 2000, a more representative year, foreign direct investment was 1.4 billion dollars, much of it from the United States but with significant participation, too, from Canada, Mexico, Europe, and Asia. For example, in 2002, the Dutch brewer Heineken invested 220 million dollars in Costa Rica. Foreign investment has contributed not just to economic growth but also to the diversity of economies. There have been significant foreign investments in such industries as electronics, computer software, "call centers," and medical equipment, as well as in textiles, food and beverages, and tourism.

The surge in export earnings—and in foreign direct investment—is employed to pay for the surge in imports. Indeed, imports have grown even faster than exports. Many goods have to be imported to support activities that generate exports. But the tractor of yesterday that was used to help with the harvest of sugarcane is more likely today to be bales of cloth to be sewn into baby clothes. The productivity and technology employed in El Salvador is said to provide for an average "value added" gain of 25 percent in the country's many textile *maquilas*. In Guatemala, Honduras, and Nicaragua, though, the gain is estimated to only be 15 percent. Thus, in these three countries, 100 million dollars' worth of textile exports necessitates 85 million dollars' worth of imports. The Intel plant in Costa Rica is said to generate more value added: the one billion dollars in exports requires 700 million dollars in imports, leaving the country with a net gain of 300 million dollars.

Many imports, however, are for consumer goods. Measuring the percentage of imports that are made up of consumer goods is difficult because countries count the importation of cars and trucks as "capital goods," a dubious decision. The importation of cars and pickup trucks has been staggering since tariffs were lowered. Many imported vehicles are second-hand cars shipped from the United States. But the sale of new cars is considerable. In 2003, for example, Costa Rica imported 130 million dollars' worth of cars from Japan alone. There are in San José, too, dealerships offering new cars from Europe and the United States: Land Rover, Mercedes Benz, BMW, Audi, Volkswagen, Volvo, Citroën, Peugeot, Ferrari, Alfa Romeo, Fiat, Skoda, General Motors, and Ford. Korean cars can be found, too, including, prominently, Hyundai. And the latest entry: Great Wall cars from China. Other countries in the isthmus offer fewer choices, but, still, there are Mercedes Benz dealerships in all five countries.

The plethora of imported goods, though, extends into every possible corner of life. There is Evian bottled water from France, Illy coffee from Italy, Sara Lee frozen bagels from the United States, Pedigree Puppy Chow from the United States, Staedtler pencils from Germany, IBM computers (with Microsoft Windows software) from the United States, Siemens telephones from Germany, and, above all, a torrent of consumer goods from China. Some goods arrive circuitously. There are, for example, inexpensive cloth gloves for workers made in Vietnam for a United States company, which, in turn, exports them to Central America. Many of these goods are sold in supermarkets or sleek shopping centers. Every major city in the region now boasts at least one mall, some of which are sizeable. These imports, and their distribution and sale, add to the diversity—the complexity— of Central America's economies. The commercial sector and the service sector are increasingly sophisticated, at least in the larger cities of the region.

Although economic liberalism—unfettered markets—has brought economic growth, those in business assert that global figures—macro-economic statistics—mask the unevenness of economic growth. There are, it is argued, "winners" and "losers" with the new economic paradigm. The winners, those who have prospered, are said to include, according to a wide range of business leaders in all five countries: banks and other financial institutions, exporters, importers, all those in tourism, and well-situated business conglomerates, many family-owned, which are able to invest in large projects, from the construction of hotels and shopping centers to plants for generating electricity. Finally, consumers, too, are said to be winners, with greater choices, improved service, and lower prices for many products.

There are "losers," though. Those economic sectors judged to be losers include: traditional agriculture, especially producers of coffee, industry, small and medium-sized firms, and low-skilled labor. The traditional agricultural sector has been hurt by low international prices. The surge of coffee production in Vietnam is held to have flooded the market, driving prices down, so far down that some coffee estates in Guatemala and Nicaragua, those with low yields, have all but been abandoned. With some other export crops, especially with sugar, there are complaints that the policies of the United States and the European Union only permit limited entry. The market for basic grains has been filled with low-cost imports—notably from the United States—undermining local production. Indeed, between 1990 and 2001, there was a decline in the acreage planted with crops for local consumption. Acreage only increased for crops destined for export. Central America now imports corn and beans, and exports asparagus and melons.

Agriculture in Guatemala, El Salvador, and Nicaragua has also suffered from the years of strife in rural areas. Agrarian reform in El Salvador and Nicaragua further disrupted agriculture. Disputes and uncertainty about land tenure led many entrepreneurs to abandon the sector altogether and retarded agricultural research and innovation. El Salvador's former vice-president Carlos Quintanilla put it poignantly when he quipped, "Salvadorans have lost their enchantment with agriculture." Though there are innovations in Guatemala's agricultural sector, Honduras and above all Costa Rica seem to have the most dynamic farmers, coming up with such novel products as purée of organic bananas (for baby food) and tubers to sell to African immigrants in the northeast of the United States. Still, much of rural Central America remains dedicated to traditional agricultural crops, sometimes with the most rudimentary of technology—the machete, the hoe, the iron-tipped wooden plow, and the ox.

Industry is another loser in Central America's economic transition to liberalism. There are, to be sure, some who have prospered, including those with a niche in the international economy. But Jorge Arriaza, a Salvadoran industrialist, captures the sentiment of many of his peers when he says, "As hard as it is to believe, it is more difficult to be an industrialist today in El Salvador than it was during our civil war." The reason—international competition. Arriaza feels that he and his Central American brethren are "between a rock and a hard place": caught between the high technology of the United States, Canada, and Europe and the low-cost labor of Asia. Where, he asks, is the space for Central America's industry? What can most efficiently be produced by industrialists in Central America? The answers are elusive.

Also hard hit by international competition, especially from Asia, are the region's many small and medium-sized firms. For example, the small Nicaraguan city of Masaya was long a center for the manufacture of shoes, carried out in small workshops. Copious imports of cheap tennis shoes from Asia have all but ended the manufacture of shoes in Masaya. Commonly, small and medium-sized firms in Central America do not have the knowledge, technology, resources, or scale to compete against imports.

Perhaps the most prominent "loser" is low-skilled labor. The transformation of Central America's economy has not generated enough jobs to absorb all those needing work. Evidence of the dearth of gainful employment can be found at the major intersections in the region's cities. In Managua there can be twenty individuals at a busy intersection, hawking a bewildering array of goods, from leather cases for cell phones to coconuts to geese.

Further evidence of inadequate job creation is in the migration of Central Americans. The numbers are startling. Here, too, is a great irony of the region's embracing of economic liberalism. The truth is that not all markets have been unfettered. Goods, services, and capital may move freely internationally. But the labor market has been rigid, bound by national borders. However, it is the migration of labor—the export of labor—that has been decisive to the economic stability of Central America. The migration of labor, mostly to the United States but also of Nicaraguans to neighboring Costa Rica (where 10 percent of the population is now believed to be Nicaraguan), is an indelible part of the liberal model.

As many as a fifth of Salvadorans have left El Salvador for the United States. They send money—remittances—"home." A study by the Inter-American Development Bank calculates that the sum sent home by Salvadorans in 2003 was 2.3 billion dollars. In marked contrast: earnings from the country's principal export—coffee—was only 105 million dollars, and the country's second most significant export—sugar—only generated 47 million dollars. El Salvador's remittances, overwhelmingly sent from the United States, are said to be equivalent to 14 percent of the country's gross national product (GNP). Coincidentally, the country's deficit in its foreign trade is nearly identical: the equivalent of 15 percent of GNP. Remittances from Salvadorans who have left the country clearly help pay for imports. They probably, too, help sustain the country's productive activities, providing, if only indirectly, necessary financial liquidity.

Guatemala's gain from remittances is also enormous: 2.1 billion dollars in 2003—equivalent to 80 percent of the country's exports. Nicaragua's remittances for the year are calculated to have been 788 million dollars, exceeding by a healthy margin the value of the country's exports. Nicaragua differs from El Salvador and Guatemala in that not all remittances are sent from the United States; many Nicaraguans are living and working in Costa Rica, from where they send funds to family members back in Nicaragua. El Salvador, Guatemala, and Nicaragua are the three countries that were embroiled in civil wars during the

1980s. The protagonists in the three countries were committed, among other aims, to curtailing the economic influence of the United States in their respective countries. Ironically, however, the conflicts only enhanced economic links with the United States. Most telling is El Salvador's decision to accept the dollar as "legal tender" and to permit it to circulate freely. The dollar is for all practical purposes now the "official"—"national"— currency of the country.

Remittances are important in Honduras, too. In 2003, Honduras received 862 million dollars in remittances. It is suggestive that Costa Rica, the most prosperous country of the isthmus, receives the lowest amount of remittances: 306 million dollars in 2003, equivalent to only 5 percent of its exports. Moreover, the figure of 306 million dollars is a gross figure; Costa Rica attracts migrants, overwhelmingly from Nicaragua, but also from Colombia and even Argentina, who send funds "home." The net "earning" from remittances in Costa Rica is estimated to have been only 100 million dollars in 2003.

The flight of so many Central Americans from their homes— their communities, their countries—is a reminder that the transformation of the region's economy has been insufficient. Poverty is pervasive in the isthmus. Indeed, a United Nations report published in 2003 concluded that one out of two Central Americans lacks the economic resources to live a life of dignity. Twenty-three percent of Central Americans were reported to be living in extreme poverty (of whom 77 percent reside in rural areas). There is a significant range, however, in this incidence of extreme poverty, from less than a tenth of the population in Costa Rica to over a third of the population in Honduras. Another indicator cited in the same report, satisfaction of basic needs (housing, potable water, sanitation, education, and purchasing power), concluded that the most needy country was Nicaragua, with 73 percent of households not having these basic needs met. This poverty would be worse if not for the remittances from family members who have emigrated.

In sum, Central America is at peace, the economies of the countries of the region are stable and growing, albeit modestly.

Growth continued even when the world economy slowed at the end of the 1990s and only haltingly limped into the twenty-first century. The economies of the region are more diverse, decidedly less dependent on the export of traditional agricultural exports. Entrepreneurs and managers are increasingly savvy, competing in the international economy. Local markets are awash in imported goods and services, enhancing choices and contributing, further, to the diversity of the region's economies.

Moreover, the region is increasingly integrated by commerce. Indeed, intra-regional trade came close to quadrupling between 1990 and 2000. The percentages of exports that are destined for another country in the isthmus are 36, 29, and 24 for Guatemala, El Salvador, and Costa Rica, respectively—relatively high percentages. (In contrast, for Honduras and Nicaragua the percentage of trade that is intra-regional is only 8 and 6 percent, respectively.) The search for economies of scale is also leading many previously national firms to invest in building a regional presence.

Still, Central America faces widespread and stubborn poverty. It is more dependent on the economic cushion provided by remittances than is commonly acknowledged. Judging the economic performance of the region is inevitably normative, depending in large measure on the basis for comparison. Also tricky is evaluating how the economic transformation of the countries of the region is shaping society. Are nations—societies—being strengthened or weakened by economic growth and heightened economic complexity and integration into the world economy? Are states being strengthened or weakened? The questions are rarely posed in the region and, in any case, the answers are far from clear.

What does seem apparent, though rarely discussed, is how poverty in the region is viewed. Formerly, when agriculture was so dominant, the rural poor majority was judged to be a link in the chain of wealth creation. They either labored for little on agricultural estates that generated exports or produced food crops to feed—at low cost—urban residents. The urban poor were migrants, fleeing rural misery, providing "services" to the well-heeled, or simply casting about, looking for some assistance. The welfare of the poor and the prosperous was irrevocably linked—a politically charged view.

The perception is different now. Instead, there is the attitude—usually unspoken—that "you are either in the market or you are not in the market." The suggested antidote to poverty is—far from looking to politics—that you find something desired by the "market," even if it is only your disposition to toil abroad (where, when you clean offices in Maryland, you still are metaphorically picking coffee beans in Matagalpa). The market is omnipresent. Those outside the market might as well disappear.

The entrepreneurs and managers who have in an atomistic and largely anonymous fashion led the transformation of Central America's economies are sober and guarded. The "opening" of the economies has created interesting opportunities but also evident threats. Emblematic, perhaps, is the experience of a Guatemalan long involved in the coffee business, Dieter Notteböhm. He had a profitable factory making jute sacks for coffee. The lowering of tariffs in Central America led to the importation of jute sacks made in Pakistan and selling for prices well below Notteböhm's cost of production. Notteböhm could not compete and had to close his factory. But he perceived an opportunity with the cultivation of macadamia nuts. He planted macadamia nut trees on his coffee estates in the highlands of Guatemala. He has done well—has profited—because he can undercut macadamia nut farmers in Hawaii who have higher costs. So goes the market.

Sheer necessity has forced the region's entrepreneurs and managers to innovate. There has been a scramble to be competitive, including among the region's many family firms. As a banker said in Honduras, "Grandmother can no longer be on the board of directors." Firms are making investments, in technology and in education and training; they are reorganizing themselves; they seek assistance from consultants; they look for niches to fill in the local, regional, and world economy; they focus their activities; they seek alliances; and they seek economies of scale. The need to be competitive has forced members of the private sector to be well informed, to know what is going on, and to have the capacity to make judgments and decisions.

With the exception perhaps of El Salvador, where the political party ARENA has deep roots in the private sector, the private sector of Central America is removed from politics. Prominent members of the private sector "pop up," emerging as candidates for public office. There is lobbying, too. But as a whole, the private sector remains distant, even wary of politics. Public life is seen as being dominated by a political class, a sect of individuals who move from leadership positions in political parties to appointments in government bureaucracies to elected office. The private sector has noted that the politicians who ushered in, with great fanfare, unfettered markets, are now gone, with many of them discredited—a few even in prison.

There is an uncertainty—a curiosity—of where the next generation of politicians, those elected to the highest office, will take the countries of the region. It is surprising, though, that given that the private sector is the "motor" of economic growth, of the generation of wealth and the creation of employment, that the private sector does not have a stronger voice in political decisions. Alberto Trejos, a colleague who served a stint as minister of foreign trade in Costa Rica, notes: "The private sector of Central America is timid. But its reserve is incompatible with its importance to the welfare of the region."

Perhaps the timidity is an inheritance from the turmoil of the 1980s. Or perhaps the timidity is a defense against the acrimonious give and take of day-to-day democracy. In any case, it is notable that liberalism in Central America, true to its philosophical underpinnings, has resulted in an atomization of public life, of the absence of a coherent sense of national purpose and national direction—of economies guided by anything other than the notorious "invisible hand." *Para bien o para mal.*

WHAT WENT RIGHT?

Like everywhere else, billboards in Costa Rica come and go. At the beginning of 2005, there was a huge billboard greeting travelers on the Pan-American Highway as they approached the Pacific coast showing a pretty girl drinking milk; its patriotic caption read: "The milk of always . . . the milk of us, the Costa Ricans—Dos Pinos." At the top of the billboard there was a Costa Rican flag and another patriotic pitch: "Proud to be 100 percent Costa Rican. International Quality." Another billboard showed five photos of smiling individuals. The caption: "This is the national insurance company . . . of Costa Ricans." Such prosaic displays of nationalism are suggestive of the pride of Costa Ricans, a pride grounded not only in a sense of distinctiveness but also of national accomplishment.

The pride of Costa Ricans has a basis. The great scourge of Latin America is inequality. But according to the World Bank, Costa Rica has less inequality than any country in Latin America except Uruguay. Perhaps it is not a coincidence either, that Costa Rica and Uruguay are the two countries in the region where public opinion polls by the Chilean firm Latinobarómetro show the highest level of support for "democracy"—with the reigning model of government. Social indicators are impressive, too. The United Nations ranks Costa Rica as having a "high level of human development." The percentage of the population judged to have access to essential medical care and medicines is 95 to 100 percent. Ninety-six percent of those fifteen and older are literate.

Life expectancy is seventy-eight years—a year more than the United States.

Costa Rica is not a rich country, but the per capita income is the highest by far in Central America and higher than the per capita incomes of Panama, Venezuela, Colombia, Ecuador, and Peru. (The per capita incomes of the Southern Cone countries— Uruguay, Argentina, and Chile—are higher than that of Costa Rica.) The difference between the per capita income of Costa Rica and its immediate neighbor to the north—Nicaragua—is especially striking. The World Bank estimates the per capita income of Costa Rica is six times that of Nicaragua; the Economic Commission for Latin America and the Caribbean (ECLAC) assesses it to be nearly eight times that of Nicaragua. Costa Rica's per capita income is also notably higher than those of other countries in Central America. It is twice as high as that of El Salvador, two and half times as high as that of Guatemala, and five times greater than that of Honduras.

Costa Rica's unemployment rate is consistently low. Indeed, the hard labor of harvesting coffee and sugarcane in Costa Rica is now done overwhelmingly by migrants from Nicaragua. Estimates vary for the percentage of Costa Ricans trapped in poverty, but the incidence of poverty is decidedly less than that of other countries on the isthmus. ECLAC's data, for example, suggest that 20 percent of Costa Ricans are poor, compared with 69 percent in Nicaragua, 77 percent in Honduras, 49 percent in El Salvador, and 60 percent in Guatemala. Perhaps more suggestive are the percentages of the national populations that endure "extreme poverty"—those who can scarcely manage to feed themselves: 6 percent in Costa Rica, 33 percent in Nicaragua, 37 percent in Honduras, 14 percent in El Salvador, and 17 percent in Guatemala.

Costa Rica's broad-based economic and social development has enabled most of the country's 4.2 million inhabitants (an estimate for 2005) to live reasonably well, with their basic needs met, with opportunities to study, and—depending on their drive and abilities—with the possibility of a wide range of careers. Costa Ricans have many opportunities. They are neither worn down by numbing poverty nor forced to abandon their country in a search for self-advancement. Many Costa Ricans enjoy material comforts, sampling from domestic goods and the cornucopia of imported products. The ownership—and use—of cars is widespread.

Moreover, relative prosperity has enriched culture offerings in Costa Rica. There is cinema, theater, art, literature, and, above all, music. The September 27, 2004, issue of *La Nación* reported that Costa Ricans read 100 magazines printed in the country and 2,500 imported magazines. Every year the National Theater in San José stages an opera, drawing on local singers but also inviting a handful of talented singers from abroad. Costumes are borrowed from Chile. Operas are presented a number of evenings and are well attended by older, well-heeled Costa Ricans. Every year, too, there are musical festivals all across San José, including one held in an abandoned train station, featuring theater and music groups from throughout the world that appeal to a young audience. The IX International Art Festival held in 2004 brought performers from Mexico, Spain, Israel, Argentina, Uruguay, Brazil, Colombia, Nicaragua, and El Salvador.

Costa Rica's prosperity is largely recent. The country has fared well with liberalism, with democracy, and with a market economy open to the world economy. Costa Rica is widely viewed, including prominently within Central America, as a "success." Between 1960 and 1969, Costa Rica's share of Central America's exports of goods was 17 percent—the same as Nicaragua. Between 1980 and 1989, Costa Rica's share of the region's exports climbed to 28 percent, while Nicaragua's share fell to 9 percent. The figures for the period 2000–2003, not including the exports of *maquilas* (and earnings from tourism), gave Costa Rica 30 percent of the region's exports of goods, compared to 8 percent for Nicaragua. However, Costa Rica has not just developed a healthy mix of goods to export; the country has also developed since the 1980s a formidable tourism industry and has attracted a significant amount of foreign investment, including for some of the more remunerative kinds of *maquilas*. Costa Rica is, in fact, the largest recipient of foreign direct investment in Central

America, attracting 30 percent of the region's foreign direct investment in 2000, a representative year.

The development of tourism as an economic activity—and it is the largest source of foreign exchange for the country—has brought with it unanticipated advantages. Tourism in Costa Rica is largely eco-tourism, with visitors exploring all corners of the country and so contributing—at least in some measure—to the development of marginal rural areas. Between 85 and 90 percent of the country's hotels have forty rooms or fewer, further diffusing the gains from tourism. The realization of the value of the country's natural resources for tourism has assisted conservation efforts. (Twenty-seven percent of the country's national territory is either enclosed in a national park or otherwise protected.) Tourism has thus been good for Costa Rica.

Costa Rica has also benefited from attracting foreign investment. The plum was the decision by Intel in 1996 to establish a manufacturing plant in the country. Intel was wooed by many countries, including Brazil, Chile, Mexico, Thailand, Indonesia, and the Philippines, but the company selected Costa Rica. By 2000, Intel had invested 400 million dollars and had 2,200 employees, including 500 professionals (mostly engineers). Other high-technology companies have followed Intel. Indeed, Costa Rica has a fledging computer software industry. There are more than 100 firms in the country writing programs, thirty of which export their products. In 2003, these exports totaled the respectable sum of 70 million dollars.

There are also successes in the manufacture of medical devices and in biotechnology. In 1998, Abbott Laboratories established a sophisticated 60-million-dollar manufacturing plant in the country. More than a dozen companies are manufacturing medical devices in Costa Rica, and their exports are significant, too.

Another example of the dynamism of the Costa Rican economy is research on pharmaceuticals and biotechnology by local institutions. This research is financed by an impressive array of foreign firms, including: Pfizer, Bayer, Bristol-Myers Squibb, Eli Lilly, MSD, Roche, and Schering. Prominent local research institutions include: the National Biodiversity Institute, the Costa Rican Institute of Clinic Investigations, and Neeman Medical. These institutions draw on talent emerging from the country's many universities, both public and private. At Costa Rica's universities there are said to be, for example, a total of sixty-seven academic programs related to biotechnology.

Costa Rica's economy is also notable for what is now largely absent: subsistence farmers barely eking out a living growing maize and beans in a setting bereft of any infrastructure except that provided by nature. Economic gains have made it possible to reduce considerably the incidence of poverty throughout the country. Even in the most remote regions of Costa Rica there are potable water, sanitation facilities, electricity—and public schools. It is revealing what Costa Ricans say when asked why, in comparison with other countries in the region, there are so few Costa Ricans who have emigrated to the United States. The answer is invariably, "Costa Rica works (*funciona*)—there is no reason to leave."

Why has Costa Rica fared so well with liberalism—with democracy and unfettered markets? How was Costa Rica able to not only diversify and strengthen its economy but to reduce the incidence of poverty by 50 percent between 1982 and 2002—in only two decades? What went right? Costa Rica has benefited enormously from political stability, from years of uninterrupted investments in public services, prominently in education and health, and from strong institutions. The country has benefited, too, from its location, for its political exceptionalism, for being the first in many economic endeavors, from foreign assistance (at a critical moment), and from the influx of many talented refugees, immigrants, and long-term visitors. These healthy "advantages" or "traits," some of which are given and others of which have been cultivated, have often reinforced one another. There is momentum in political and economic development—good things appear to entice or beget other good things.

Costa Rica has not always enjoyed political stability. From 1824 to 1899, the presidency changed hands on average every two and a half years. Thirty-seven presidents resigned before completing their terms, and another 20 percent were ousted by the military. From 1835 to 1899, the country had six different constitutions, but nonetheless over half the time the country was just ruled by a general. In 1889, political parties emerged and elections became routine. However, voting was highly restrictive, with only about 15 percent of adults eligible to cast ballots. Political parties were little more than personalistic electoral tools, and electoral fraud was common. Politics was dominated by affluent, charismatic, but domineering individuals and their cronies. Moreover, of the twenty presidents who served between 1890 and 1948, four were installed through force, four were imposed by incumbent presidents, and four more took office through elite compromises that subverted elections. Ideas about politics and economics, usually draped in the garb of conservative and liberal phraseology, had little import.

In 1940, though, the candidate of what had been a drab, moderate political party, the National Republican Party, Rafael Ángel Calderón, won the elections, formed a coalition with those on the "left," and began a series of social reforms that have had an indelible impact on Costa Rica. Calderón, said to have been influenced by his studies in Belgium, pushed a reform agenda that led to the establishment of a social security system and the creation of a public university in 1941. In 1942, the constitution was amended to establish a set of social guarantees. In 1943, a labor code was codified that guaranteed a minimum wage, an eight-hour workday, basic safety and sanitation conditions in the workplace, the right to form unions, and even the right to housing. These progressive reforms promised to improve social welfare, but they also inflicted a heavy burden on the state. Government expenditures came close to doubling in just three years, from 1940 to 1943. Evidence of fiscal mismanagement aggravated fears inspired by a growing budget deficit, an empowered labor force, and the influence of the "left."

Calderón's handpicked candidate won election in 1944, though, and reforms continued. Still, the economy was dominated by two crops—coffee and bananas—which generated 90 percent of the country's foreign exchange. It was said, for all the talk of politics, that "the best minister of finance is a good coffee harvest."

The campaign for the presidency in 1948 loomed as a major turning point in Costa Rica. Disputed election returns followed a violent campaign. The opposition appeared to have won the election, but the incumbent party controlled congress, and it self-servingly voted to annul the elections. Rebellion erupted. The principal opposition was a group called National Liberation, led by José Figueres. Fighting stopped; negotiations ensued; the outcome was a junta headed by Figueres that governed for a year and a half. Figueres outlawed the Communist Party and dealt harshly with leftist leaders who sought to organize and rally Costa Ricans. No surprise. But at the same time Figueres nationalized the Costa Rican banks, placed a 10 percent tax on private capital to pay for administrative changes, promoted agricultural production and the development of new energy resources, and began dissolving the Costa Rican army. The possibility of radical change was nipped in the bud—there would be no social revolution in Costa Rica—but Calderón's social reforms continued.

In 1952, Figueres won the presidency outright. His National Liberation Party promised a broad program of social and economic reform. Figueres and his party kept their promises: income taxes were raised; labor benefits were enhanced; and to protect and promote industry, tariffs were raised. There were complaints of demagoguery and charges of corruption, however. An anecdote that still circulates tells of Figueres being asked about a missing sum of money. When asked what he had done with the funds, he replied: "I bought candy and ate it. So what?" (*Me los comí en confites. ¿Y qué?*).

The opposition did not get eliminated or bought off. In what became a feature of Costa Rica's democracy, the presidency began to rotate between two dominant but inclusive political parties. In the 1960s, with the heady debates that were taking place elsewhere in Latin America about economic development, the focus of political debate in Costa Rica increasingly centered on how the small country could best participate in the international economy, and the respective roles of the state and the private sector in spurring growth and "modernization." What emerged was an eclectic yet pragmatic hodgepodge of initiatives that assigned a vigorous role for the state in the economy, but without a disdain for the private sector. The labor force was respected, healthy, educated, and nurtured.

In 1963, Costa Rica entered the Central American Common Market, an attempt to foster industrialization by creating a sheltered market for the region's "infant industries." The aspiration was to escape the existing dependence on exports of agricultural commodities by "substituting" imported industrial and consumer goods with items produced locally. If you imported less, the reasoning went, you could likewise export less. The common market worked well—for Costa Rica, anyway—until 1969. It worked less well subsequently, in part because of tension between El Salvador and Honduras. The sharp rise in petroleum prices in the early 1970s put stress on Costa Rica's balance of payments, but like elsewhere in Latin America, the burden was largely masked by foreign borrowing. Still, the commercial imbalance was worrisome. Costa Rican authorities were seemingly prescient, though, in creating already in 1968 the Center for the Promotion of Exports and Investments (CENPRO). The Center's efforts were given a boost in 1972 with the establishment of the Law to Promote Exports, which offered financial benefits to those who exported non-traditional goods (and those who exported to non-traditional markets).

The economy remained vulnerable, however. Foreign debt grew, the result of excessive borrowing abroad to meet the difference between higher prices for oil and other imports and lower prices for coffee and other exports. Moreover, the government had to subsidize state enterprises that were also established in 1972, state-owned utilities, as well as a panoply of social welfare programs. The triumph of the Sandinista Revolution in 1979 in neighboring Nicaragua unnerved the economy and was the end of what had anyway become a nearly moribund, limp Central American Common Market. Adding to the financial pressure was a worldwide recession. The Costa Rican economy entered into a period of crisis in 1980: the currency, the *colón*, was sharply devalued; inflation skyrocketed; unemployment rose; and salaries adjusted for inflation fell by 30 percent. (Not surprisingly, calculations of per capita consumption also suggested a decline of 30 percent.) In 1982, the government had to declare a moratorium on the payment of its foreign debt. The situation looked bleak indeed.

The 1982 presidential election was won by Luis Alberto Monge. He was skillful in securing substantial aid and support from the United States and the international banking community. But the United States was also keen on helping Costa Rica, to present it as an alternative model to revolutionary Nicaragua. The United States provided significant direct assistance, much of it channeled through the United States Agency for International Development (USAID), and it also facilitated support from international financial organizations such as the World Bank, the International Monetary Fund, and the Inter-American Development Bank. Some assistance was in the form of direct monetary transfers—used to ease pressure on the balance of payments. Other assistance took the form of guidance in restructuring the economy, removing "market distortions" and encouraging entrepreneurship within the private sector, especially that which led to exports. Although the rhetoric of the United States suggested a quick and ruthless reform of the economy, aid officials were, while insistent, pragmatic and patient, respecting political realities. At times they led the Costa Rican private sector into businesses that would compete directly against United States producers.

What emerged in Costa Rica was not an abrupt embracing of economic liberalism—of unfettered markets—but instead a slow, gradual reform. Some market distortions were removed, but others remained to protect well-established but vulnerable sectors of the economy. To stimulate entrepreneurial activity, generous subsidies were granted to those who exported. Some Costa Ricans look back and say the subsidies were "obscene" and that anyone—or any private sector—would have responded. Still, it was notable—and even crucial—that the private sector did, in fact, respond. While the private sector in Costa Rica was nervous about the Sandinista Revolution and about insurrections in El Salvador and Guatemala, it was "safe"; there were no threats to property or to personal security. The private sector of Costa Rica was able to respond effectively to a mix of cajoling, new opportunities, and material incentives.

International assistance, most of it either directly or indirectly coming from the United States, provided guidance and financial support. All of the countries of Latin America were rocked by the economic crises of the 1980s, but on a per capita basis, no country in the region received as much assistance as Costa Rica. Costa Rica also surely benefited in the 1980s from the influx of capital from Nicaragua seeking a safe haven and from well-heeled and talented Nicaraguans who perceived the Sandinistas to be a threat to their interests and relocated, at least temporarily, in Costa Rica.

Costa Rican entrepreneurs were the first in Central America to probe around international markets, looking for niches to exploit. They found such products to export as ornamental plants, herbs, palm hearts, melons, and pineapples. In these endeavors they benefited from being first, for getting "a leg up in the market," and from the higher prices that greet new products. By the time that other Central Americans (or South Americans) entered these niches, the Costa Ricans were either skilled at controlling costs and quality, or had ensconced themselves into markets—or had moved on to other, more lucrative endeavors. Likewise, a continued stream of refugees, migrants, and long-term visitors stimulated entrepreneurial activity. The country's best-known brand of coffee, sold as far away as China, is Café Britt—the successful product of an American expatriate who founded the company in 1985. Costa Rica's small size, smugness, and political stability earned it the nickname "the Switzerland of Latin America." Some say, though, that it is better described as "the United States of Latin America" for its heady mixture of political stability, strong institutions, relative prosperity, and hard-working and imaginative immigrants.

The president who succeeded Luis Alberto Monge, Óscar Arias, labored hard for a negotiated settlement to the conflicts in the region. For his efforts, he was awarded the Nobel Prize for Peace in 1987. The award, and accompanying publicity, helped consolidate Costa Rica's image as a "peaceful" country: an image that proved to be invaluable for the promotion of tourism, which has come to be the country's most lucrative industry. Costa Rica surely saved resources by disbanding its armed forces in the aftermath of the 1948 conflict, though the country still spends considerable funds on "national defense." The absence of a military has reinforced the perception of Costa Rica as being a peaceful, stable country, an image that has attracted tourists—and foreign investment. Tourists buy shirts labeled "Armed Forces of Costa Rica" adorned with macaws (the air force), dolphins (the navy), and ants (the army). It is quipped in Guatemala, and perhaps elsewhere, that there are two great marketing successes in Latin America: the Colombian coffee of Juan Valdez and the peace of Costa Rica. Similarly, though perhaps mean-spirited, is the observation that "Costa Rica benefited from war in the 1980s and from peace in the 1990s."

When tourists began to arrive in mass in the 1990s, they encountered more than peace: they encountered infrastructure, including national parks and museums. The parks and the museums are two examples of Costa Rica's ability to build and sustain institutions that contribute to economic growth, even if that was not the intention at the moment of their inception. In the late 1960s, there was a global initiative, led, it is said, by biologists, to establish national parks in unique habitats. Costa Rica's universities support a substantial number of biologists who successfully lobbied for the establishment of a network of national parks in the country. The intent was conservation. A parallel effort led to the establishment of three prominent museums in the country: the National Museum, the Pre-Columbian Gold Museum, and (as it is commonly called) the Jade Museum. All three museums house collections of pre-Columbian artifacts that represent the cultural patrimony of the country. Again, the intent was conservation. However, these institutions, and the national parks in particular, proved invaluable with the emergence—and cultivation—of the tourist industry.

Thus, in summary, Costa Rica's success in revamping its economy since the crisis of 1980–1982 can be traced to the confluence of a number of factors: strategic location; long-standing investments in public welfare, education in particular; political stability; strong institutions; a private sector with incentives to respond to a new model of economic development; foreign guidance and assistance; a gradual, pragmatic—and even incomplete—embracing of economic liberalism; the advantage of being first in many economic endeavors; and getting a boost from those attracted to the country's many charms.

Perhaps, though, these explanations of Costa Rica's success are superficial. Scientists might say that these are "intervening variables," that there are deeper social forces at work. Is there something intrinsic to Costa Rica or to Costa Ricans as a people, a nation, that has led inexorably to political stability, the creation of strong institutions—which serve as the foundation of the polity—and a commitment to public welfare, to the education and health of the population? Many Costa Ricans, including prominently intellectuals, say yes: the root of Costa Rican's success is the country's social equality.

Costa Rica's history is interpreted as having been conducive to the creation of a society—a nation—that was, at its core, egalitarian. Indigenous groups fiercely resisted Spanish colonialism, but either their numbers were small or they were quickly decimated. There were no apparent riches, and the area was of slight importance to Spain. The absence of an indigenous population that could be exploited for its labor largely precluded the chance of constructing a rigid social hierarchy. There was no reason, either, to import African slaves in any number, though there were some slaves, and Costa Ricans of African descent were not granted the right to vote until 1949.

In the mythology of the nation, Costa Rica was settled largely by yeoman farmers. By the 1830s, when the cultivation of coffee began to flower, the social framework of the country was set, and even though some estates—and fortunes—emerged, the economy was still characterized by small, independent farms. This "rural democracy," it is argued, spawned not just a tradition of resolving conflicts through legal and administrative channels, but also a social culture of respect for all and a suspicion of grandeur.

The words of Miguel Ángel Rodríguez, who served as president of Costa Rica from 1998 to 2002, are instructive. In an interview published in *The New Leader* in late 2002, just after leaving office, Rodríguez said of Costa Rica:

> This is a country of egalitarians (*igualados*). Costa Ricans do not accept that anyone is superior. We do not have the American celebration of success. We prefer to be loved—or liked—rather than successful. If someone is perceived to be acting superior we say, "the floor needs to be lowered"—and there are many ways to do that, including with satire and ridicule.
>
> There is a story of a wealthy Costa Rican, Fernando Castro, who in the 1930s had a ranch in the northwest of the country that bordered the tracks of the national railroad. Don Fernando took the train to and from his ranch. Annoyed by the heat, he asked the railroad's directors why they didn't plant trees along the tracks to offer shade. The directors replied that they had no money. Don Fernando said he would pay for the planting of trees. The directors said no, they would not have money for the care of them. Don Fernando said he would establish a fund for the pruning of the trees. The directors said no, because they suspected he was planning to profit from his gesture. The trees were never planted.
>
> When I was president I could get in my car on the weekend and drive anywhere, with no security personnel. People would recognize me and be kind, but I was considered just another Costa Rican. If I wanted to go to the movies, I waited in line like everyone else.

Rodríguez' portrayal of Costa Rica's social equality is persuasive. There are many characteristics—or customs—in Costa Rica that are likewise suggestive. Those hailing a taxi, for example, commonly sit up front, next to the driver, so they can converse. In neighboring Nicaragua, where class distinctions are pronounced, passengers sit in the back of the taxi. Waiters are less subservient in Costa Rica than in other Central American countries. The wealthy in Costa Rica tend to be less ostentatious then their brethren elsewhere in the isthmus.

Even the tragic fate of Rodríguez is revealing. On September 15, 2004, Rodríguez assumed the position of secretary general of the Organization of American States (OAS), having been elected by thirty-four representatives of the nation-states of the Americas. He was the first Central American elected to the prestigious post. But back in Costa Rica evidence surfaced suggesting he had received over a million dollars in "commissions" (kickbacks) from the French telecommunications company Alcatel in exchange for a lucrative contract awarded to the company. The Costa Rican authorities issued an international warrant for Rodríguez' arrest. After only seventeen days in his plush Washington, D.C., office, Rodríguez resigned from the OAS. He returned to Costa Rica at his own volition, flying first class. But on his arrival at San José's airport, on October 15, the police slapped handcuffs on him, put him in the back of a paddy wagon, and took him to a courtroom for booking. Costa Ricans applauded the authorities. The sentiment abounded that "if a man caught stealing a chicken is thrown in prison, then a corrupt politician should also be thrown in prison." Rodríguez had "the floor lowered."

Costa Rica's social equality—matched with the country's benign distribution of income—is real. But how consequential is it? What is the link between, as one Nicaraguan put it, "Costa Rica's fetish for equality" and Costa Rica's recent success in the international economy? Many believe that social equality is a good thing, that it is an end in and of itself, but it is not easy to understand, for example, how social equality could stimulate entrepreneurial activity. Maybe homogeneous nations suffer from less social conflict and so are better able to provide the strong institutions and political stability that seem to be necessary, though hardly sufficient, prerequisites for economic development. That interpretation seems plausible, but is it credible? Perhaps. What seems safest, though, is identifying the most immediate national characteristics—and decisions—that at any one moment in time contribute to economic development. The weight of history and culture is real, but it is uncertain, and it is certainly not deterministic.

Costa Ricans are aware that they have navigated successfully the shoals of an economic transformation, that the country is prosperous and at peace. But every step forward brings new challenges. There are always concerns. Costa Ricans now worry less about poverty and instead about social cohesion, which seems threatened by the rapidity of economic change, materialism, rising crime, large numbers of migrants, and other sweeping forces. Worse, these challenges seem beyond the control of traditional institutions: family, church, political parties, and the state itself.

The indictment of Miguel Ángel Rodríguez was not an isolated event. Two other former presidents also fell under suspicion of corruption: they are the sons of the two "founding fathers"; both bear their father's names, and they served back-to-back as presidents. Rafael Ángel Calderón served as president from 1990 to 1994; José María Figueres served as president from 1994 to 1998. Their tarnished images are a blow to public esteem and to the standing of the two political parties that have served as a bedrock of Costa Rica's democracy: the National Liberation Party (of Figueres) and the Social Christian Unity Party (of Rodríguez and Calderón). There are fears of an electoral "dealignment" and even of the discrediting of the economic model, of markets open to competition.

Indeed, in the 2006 presidential election the governing party, the Social Christian Unity Party, won less than 4 percent of the vote. The candidate of the National Liberation Party, Óscar Arias, barely eked out a victory, with a margin of only 1.2 percent. The election was so close that the Supreme Tribunal of Elections spent more than three weeks manually recounting all of the ballots. A strong challenge was made by the upstart candidate of the Citizen Action Party, Ottón Solis. That Arias, with his stature as a former president and winner of the Nobel Prize for Peace, did not trounce Solis came as a shock. A disgruntled Costa Rican quipped, "The Social Christian Unity Party is dead, and the National Liberation Party is on artificial respiration."

Costa Rica will have to make hard decisions about the future direction of the country: nation-states are always reinventing themselves, all the more so at times of stress. These decisions about the future course of the country, though, will be shaped in large part by the history—the culture—of Costa Rica, as well as by the understood possibilities for the future.

WHAT WENT WRONG?

Beginning in 1936, Nicaragua was effectively headed by General Anastasio Somoza and his family for more than four decades. In January 1951, his government requested the World Bank to send a general survey mission to the country to assist in spurring economic development. The World Bank complied, sending a special mission, which was stationed in Nicaragua from July 1951 to May 1952. The team conducted interviews, reviewed data, and had a firsthand look at the infrastructure of the country. The outlook was deemed promising. In addition to Nicaragua being the largest but least densely populated country in Central America, the World Bank mission was impressed with the commitment of the Nicaraguan government to economic progress:

> From its nearly year-long travel in the country, the mission concluded that few underdeveloped countries have so great a physical potential for growth and economic development as does Nicaragua. . . . it has almost unlimited land for development. . . . The physical resources of the country provide a sound basis for economic development. . . . During the past two years the government has shown a clear awareness of the need for improvement and of the areas where improvement is necessary. It has demonstrated both the imagination and will to move forward with vigorous action. Economic

conditions have reinforced the determination of the government. During the past two years, the economic and financial position of the country has been stronger than ever before. The national income has never been higher. These conditions, together with the administrative changes being undertaken by the government, can provide the stimulus for very rapid economic development and a promising future.

The staff of the World Bank was thus confident that Nicaragua was primed for an economic takeoff, an accelerated period of growth that would "modernize" the country. What was missing was a suitable program—or plan—backed by foreign assistance. The World Bank itself was prepared to meet these needs: it offered a plan and assistance. Emphasis was placed in the plan on further developing the agricultural sector and on improving infrastructure, including transportation, vital to agricultural growth. The plan also embraced investments in industry and power and in education and public health. Concessionary loans were offered to implement the sweeping program.

The government—or regime—of Anastasio Somoza complied with the recommendations of the World Bank, and his dynastic descendants, sons Luis and Anastasio, likewise followed the suggestions of succeeding World Bank missions. Just as predicted, economic growth ensued. Acreage planted increased, with the "agricultural frontier" being pushed farther and farther away from long-settled areas. New crops—such as cotton, beef, tobacco, and sesame seeds—helped diversify the "agro-export economy," as it was labeled. The public sector dedicated itself to strengthening the country's infrastructure and to assisting the initiatives of the private sector.

The Nicaraguan economy flourished. During the first half of the 1950s, in fact, the economy grew at an annual rate of 9 percent, although in the second half of the decade annual growth was only 2.5 percent. Then between 1960 and 1970, annual growth rates increased to 7.3 percent. Moreover, there was price stability, and the national currency—the *córdoba*—held its value against the dollar. By 1970, per capita income had tripled from what it had been measured to be by the World Bank in its 1952 report, even though the population had doubled in the twenty-year period. (Nicaragua had a very high population growth rate throughout the twentieth century.)

The growth of agricultural exports was blamed by some for curtailing access to fertile lands long worked by peasants. Others, though, point out that the area dedicated to the cultivation of the traditional crops of Nicaraguan peasants—white corn and red beans—did not diminish during the 1950s and, in fact, increased significantly during the 1960s. The number of farms in the country doubled between 1952 and 1970, from 51,000 to 117,000 farms. Only 1,500 farms were larger than 500 *manzanas* (roughly 350 hectares or 875 acres). In the agricultural export sector, by 1970 there were 7,000 cotton producers, 25,000 coffee producers, and 40,000 ranchers raising cattle.

Still, there was poverty in rural Nicaragua. Rural workers, generally landless, constituted over half of the economically active rural population but received—by some estimations—less than 10 percent of the total gross value of output. The second-largest rural group consisted of self-employed and family labor. Here, some fared well, others not. Access to land was sometimes contested, but, in general, land was not a driving force for social change. Even for the mystical guerrilla figure from the early part of the twentieth century, Augusto César Sandino, land in Nicaragua was abundant, and there were no parallels between his guerrilla movement, which opposed United States intervention and occupation of the country, and the Mexican Revolution, whose essence he held to be "agrarian." Indeed, during the 1950s and 1960s, Nicaragua's small farmers became fortified, and they would become the backbone—the "social base"—of the counter-revolution in the 1980s.

Early in the morning of December 23, 1972, a tremendous earthquake leveled Managua. More than 10,000 Nicaraguans lost their lives; many more were injured. Three-fourths of the buildings of the city, from the National Cathedral to modest residences, were destroyed. In addition to the loss of life and material damage, the country—it has been said—was "decapitated." The earthquake was just ill fortune, no fault of Nicaraguans. However, the country's loss was multifaceted and immense.

Despite the damage wrought by the earthquake, the Nicaraguan economy continued to grow. Indeed, the annual growth rate between 1971 and 1977 was 6 percent. By 1977, more than 50 percent of the population was urban—the highest percentage in Central America. There were continued advances in the provision of social services, including health care. Also impressive is the increase in students: the number of children enrolled in primary schools between 1965 and 1977 increased from 215,000 to 390,000; high school enrollment jumped during the same period from 25,000 to more than 100,000. The number of university students increased fivefold, reaching 24,000 in 1977. In summary, twenty-five years of growth, from 1952 to 1977, changed not only the economy, but also the social structure of the country.

What remained constant was the political regime, unchanged since 1936, a distant era when most Nicaraguans lived in the countryside and did not look much beyond their fences. In the cities there were those who labored in commerce, the public sector, and a few professionals—mostly doctors and lawyers. Nicaragua did not have business associations, unions, or even a "middle class"—none of the social actors who could have been expected to shake off the *ancien régime,* until, paradoxically, it opted to facilitate their emergence through economic policies recommended by the World Bank.

The Somoza family, father and sons (and cousins, nephews, nieces, wives, and mistresses), initiated the economic and social modernization of Nicaragua, but they were not willing to modernize the political regime. In this process new economic and social actors emerged with a desire for a democratic opening of the country, for a more "modern," "efficient," and "responsible" government. Moreover, support—or even tolerance—for the government was sapped by the blatant, even arrogant mismanagement

of the foreign assistance provided in the aftermath of the devastating earthquake in Managua. The earthquake presented the government with an urgent and visible task. The Somoza family failed and so lost legitimacy.

The political intractability of the Somoza regime provided an opportunity for the Sandinista National Liberation Front (FSLN), created in 1961 by nine men who took Sandino as their inspiration. They found their military model in Fidel Castro's guerrilla movement, which had just two years earlier managed to seize control of Cuba. Over the years, the FSLN suffered many setbacks, but it always recuperated. By the mid-1970s, the FSLN had become divided into three factions, each with a different strategy for ousting Somoza. A spectacular seizing of the Congress in August 1978 by one faction captured the imagination of young Nicaraguans—and 60 percent of the population was eighteen or younger. The revolutionary agent proved to be neither workers nor peasants, but youth. The theater was neither factory nor mountain, but city streets. The seizure of neighborhoods—and later entire cities—by boys and girls (*los muchachos*), defiant but poorly armed, with their faces covered with handkerchiefs, was widely covered by the international media.

The Somozas were soon isolated, abandoned by their erstwhile allies, including the United States government, the local business community, and the Catholic Church. Ironically, the modernizing regime became obsolete. The National Guard, little more than a palace guard, collapsed when Anastasio Somoza, family members, and cronies, flew to Miami. On July 19, 1979, a jubilant crowd gathered in the plaza in front of the ruins of the National Cathedral to celebrate the demise of the *ancien régime*. The costs of the Revolution were immense. Still, all expected a change for the better. But what?

The Revolution was made possible by a broad coalition of opponents to the Somoza dictatorship. The Sandinistas were the armed vanguard, however, and they quickly and adroitly consolidated political power, in part by patching up their own internal differences. At the first national assembly of Sandinista cadres, held over a three-day period in September 1979, the following conclusion was reached:

> We assisted in the fusion of the crisis of capitalism with the crisis of the dictatorship, such that the crisis of the dictatorship came to be, too, the crisis of the economic system, the end of this dependent capitalism, based on the exploitation of workers. The defeat of the dictatorship by the revolutionary struggle of the masses and their vanguard (the FSLN) opens the doors, to present and implement, not just a new political system, but also—and above all—a new and distinct social-economic transition, which has to be based on revolutionary power, expressing the interests of workers, peasants, and other oppressed sectors of our society.

The Sandinistas avoided, at least in public, using the term—and phraseolology—of socialism (or communism), but they labored to put the state in control of the commanding heights of the economy.

The confiscation of the considerable assets of the Somoza family and their accomplices gave the Sandinistas a base for "social accumulation." In addition, new government decrees entrusted the state with control of banking and foreign trade, and permitted the confiscation of farms and factories from the private sector under certain circumstances (which in time became increasingly broad). The state assumed sweeping responsibilities, which were exercised by an eclectic mixture of Nicaraguans with varying degrees of preparation and political philosophies and foreigners ranging from North American academics to South American dissidents to advisors from Cuba, Bulgaria, and other countries firmly committed to state management of the economy for the purpose of building a more equitable society.

The regime became something like the Tower of Babel, but the most immediate problems were that: (1) the Nicaraguan state—the public sector, led by the Sandinistas—was overwhelmed by the magnitude and complexity of managing the economy, small and poor as it was, and (2) Sandinista policies generated much opposition from many quarters. Contradictions quickly emerged. Redistributing land from wealthy farmers to poor peasants inevitably resulted in a fall in the production of agricultural commodities for export, diminishing the flow of sorely needed foreign exchange. Alleviating unemployment by swelling the ranks of workers at state enterprises led to fiscal losses. Controlling food prices to appease poor urban consumers undermined incentives to produce food in the countryside. These kinds of disruptions in micro-economic linkages led to a devastating combination of shortages and inflation. State management of resulting problems was ineffective. For example, revisions in the price of sugar, necessitated by rising prices of inputs for cultivating sugarcane and refining it, entailed the approval of five ministries and presidential approval—taking six months—by which time any agreement was sorely out of date. The Revolution engendered not some new model of economic organization but chaos.

The Sandinista regime also provoked opposition, most prominently from the United States government, which was especially angered to learn that the FSLN was assisting its revolutionary brethren in El Salvador, the Farabundo Martí National Liberation Front (FMLN). The United States government began to provide generous funding and assistance to a counter-revolution. While remnants of Somoza's National Guard were present, what was striking about the counter-revolution was its ability to draw support from peasants angered by Sandinista agrarian policies. The social base of the Revolution came to be urban, while the social base of the counter-revolution was rural. The chief of military counter-intelligence of the Sandinista People's Army admitted as much when he said, "The countryside is counter-revolutionary" (*El campo es contra*).

Fighting the counter-revolution absorbed enormous resources from an already strained state. In 1987, between the army, militias, police, and special forces of the Ministry of Governance, the state was mobilizing—and supporting—between 170,000 and 180,000 combatants. The army alone was said to be absorbing 30 percent of the state budget, and it was estimated, too, that 50 percent of the budget was being dedicated, if only indirectly, to national defense. The pressure was asphyxiating. In 1988, inflation exceeded 33,000 percent.

The Sandinistas tried to stabilize the economy with a number of policies inspired by the International Monetary Fund, but it was too little and too late. The holding of elections in February 1990, a bid to relieve military and political as well as financial pressure on the beleaguered regime, resulted in the end of the Revolution. The Sandinista candidate, *Comandante de la Revolución* Daniel Ortega, garnered 41 percent of the votes; the opposition candidate, Violeta Barrios de Chamorro, received 55 percent of the votes. (The candidates of small parties received the remaining share of votes.)

While the decade of the 1980s was difficult for all of the Central American countries, all but Nicaragua had at least some economic growth. Nicaragua became decidedly poorer in this decade. By all measures, the decline was precipitous. Some calculations put the economy of 1990 on a par with where it had been, on a per capita basis, in 1942. Nicaragua became the second-poorest country of the Americas, only better off than Haiti.

The end of the Sandinista regime was bracketed by the collapse of socialism in the countries of Eastern Europe, in 1989, and the collapse of the Soviet Union, in 1991. Predictably, within Nicaragua the Sandinista Revolution generated political and even personal animosities. Seen from afar, though, it appeared to many that Nicaragua had been demoted by a political regime that was fatally flawed. A bad choice had been made, but then, perhaps, it was the Somoza family's political intransigency, coupled with the vogue of revolution in the 1960s and 1970s among university students in poor countries, that led Nicaragua to adopt an unworkable political and economic model of governance. From this perspective, the decade of the 1980s was just a bizarre and unfortunately destructive interlude, but not a reflection of some innate characteristic of the nation-state.

The government of Violeta Barrios furthered a transition to democracy and a transition to a market economy. Both transitions proved to be difficult. Before giving up the reins of government, the Sandinistas "privatized" many state assets, from pickup trucks to farms, turning these over to themselves as individuals or to party organizations. The questionable legality of these transactions added to the many conflicts over property that had accumulated throughout the 1980s. Resolving property disputes was debilitating. Also burdensome was the reduction in the number of state employees, especially in the armed forces. Most significant, though, was a reworking of the relationship between the public and private sectors, with a significant scaling back of the role of the state, leaving the management of the economy to private initiative.

There were many problems. The economy was in shambles. Markets depend on secure property rights and the enforcement of contracts, but the Nicaraguan legal system was rickety, deterring investment. Perhaps most consequential, entrepreneurs and managers were largely absent from the economy, having long ago left the turmoil of Nicaragua and being reluctant to return. The country's exports continued as they had been in the nineteenth century, with coffee the most important source of foreign exchange.

Paradoxically, in an era of liberalism, the state, recipient of so much foreign assistance as well as loans and tax revenue, continues to be the major protagonist in the Nicaraguan economy. Indeed, it is said in Managua that "if you are not in the state budget, you are not in the middle class." Government is "the biggest business" in the country—explaining, perhaps, the continued intensity of political conflict in Nicaragua. Foreign assistance has been, in fact, crucial for the revamping of the Nicaraguan state and therefore crucial for Nicaragua as a country. Nicaragua has been the country in Latin America most favored with foreign aid, but this does not seem to have been used to jump-start the private sector into competing with new products and services in international markets. Instead, foreign aid, along with remittances, seems to have lulled the economy into a somnolence.

The commercial sector, especially in Managua, seems to thrive, but it is hard to identify new productive activities in Nicaragua, especially ones that are competitive internationally.

The poor majority of Nicaraguans struggle on, dedicated to subsistence agriculture in the countryside or doing something in the informal sector of Managua or another city (if only selling plastic bags of chilled water at intersections). Many migrate to neighboring Costa Rica to pick coffee, cut sugarcane, clean houses, serve as security guard (*guachiman*), or labor in other low-paying jobs. Nicaragua's embracing of economic liberalism has not brought much in the way of improvement for the lives of Nicaraguans. Economic growth in the 1990s was modest. There was no bounce back from the decline of the 1980s or evidence of any new, healthy trajectory of sustained economic growth.

Why? Was the country too broke and beleaguered after the Sandinista Revolution to catch up with other countries, including prominently Costa Rica, which had a head start with developing and marketing non-traditional exports? Did the country's international image of strife and lack of infrastructure constrain it from competing for the lucrative tourist market that has contributed so much to Costa Rica's prosperity? Did this international image also retard the attraction of foreign investment? Did the Sandinista Revolution chase off most entrepreneurs and managers and corrupt many of those who stayed into living off a combination of government contracts, foreign aid, and other easy money? Did continued political uncertainty—including the possible return of the Sandinistas to power—limit investment and innovation in the private sector? Answers to these questions are elusive, but the questions, when grouped together, probably point to what has gone wrong in Nicaragua.

Violeta Barrios finished her term as president and left office without insisting on her continued participation in political life. In the 1996 elections, turnout was heavy and the winner was Arnoldo Alemán, the candidate of the resurrected party of the Somozas, the Liberal Party. He had served as mayor of Managua and had used the position to build a formidable election

Varieties of Liberalism in Central America

machine, trading small favors for political support and engaging in endless self-promotion. All public works were accompanied by a sign reminding residents of Managua that he was the mayor and with his slogan: "Deeds not words" (*obras no palabras*).

What was surprising to all was the intimate relationship that Alemán developed with Daniel Ortega, who, despite having lost two consecutive elections, remained in control of the Sandinista party, the FLSN. With the control that the two leaders exerted over their party members serving in congress, they were able to modify the constitution to enable them to distribute among themselves government positions, including those in the judicial system. Nicaragua passed from being a winner-take-all presidential democracy, with a division of power among the executive, legislative, and judicial branches, to a "consociational democracy," a coalition of two political parties, firmly controlled by their leaders, in collusion for their mutual benefit. The surprise was not only the accommodation with Alemán, long known for his anti-Sandinista views. The FSLN, continued revolutionary rhetoric notwithstanding, became what some call *orteguismo*—everything was Ortega. The cadres of the FSLN either submitted to Ortega's decisions or—as many did—left the party.

The collusion between Alemán and Ortega led to petty, parochial, and corrupt governance of Nicaragua. A prominent entrepreneur with considerable investments in both Costa Rica and Nicaragua summarized in a private discussion the differences between doing business in the two countries during the administration of Alemán: "In both countries there is corruption, but in Nicaragua you need political protection to be in business, whereas in Costa Rica you do not." When asked if political protection has a cost, the answer was a predictable "Yes." Similarly, an anecdote that circulates in Managua recounts how a prominent Nicaraguan banker was obstructed by a public official known to be a Sandinista. The banker asked for a meeting with Ortega to discuss the problem. Ortega was reported to be sympathetic but to have retired from the meeting, leaving a subordinate to discuss some details. The subordinate asked for a sizeable contribution to the FSLN.

With all this wheeling and dealing, there is no serious and informed discussion, with broad participation, on how Nicaragua as an impoverished country could advance. Nicaragua has continued to have paltry economic growth, with no emergence of new industries able to compete successfully internationally. By most accounts, per capita income barely improved between 1990 and 2000. In 2000, coffee still represented 23 percent of the value of Nicaragua's exports; in neighboring Costa Rica, even with double the production, coffee only represented 5 percent of the value of the country's exports. When coffee prices fall, it is a tragedy for Nicaragua and only a nuisance for Costa Rica. During a decade of rapid economic change elsewhere in Central America, the Nicaraguan economy has remained lackluster.

The revisions of the Nicaraguan constitution did not go so far as to permit presidential reelection. In the 2001 elections, Ortega was defeated for the third consecutive time, though he still received 43 percent of the votes cast. The Sandinistas continued to hold an important block of seats in congress and an ample number of judges dispersed throughout the judicial system. The winner of the presidential elections was Arnoldo Alemán's vice-president, Enrique Bolaños. Alemán was elected to congress, and with his firm control of the Liberal Party, he set himself up to not only preside over congress, but be the equal of Bolaños.

The corruption of Alemán, though, was notorious and proved to be his undoing. In early August 2002, Bolaños denounced Alemán on radio and television, alleging the theft from state coffers of 97.6 million dollars. At one point Bolaños said, as if he were speaking directly to his predecessor—and former colleague: "Arnoldo, you took away the pensions of the retired, medicine from the nurses, paychecks from the teachers." Alemán's indictment was only made possible by a political alliance—tenuous as it may have been—between the Sandinistas and Bolaños. In time, Alemán was convicted on corruption charges and sentenced to twenty years in prison.

The Liberal Party remained, however, loyal to Alemán, keeping a distance from Bolaños. Symbolically, the framed portrait of Alemán continued to adorn the lobby of the party's national headquarters in Managua. Bolaños had to negotiate with Ortega, but every time he did the United States government objected. Ortega strengthened his hand by reconciling with his nemesis, Nicaragua's powerful cardinal, Miguel Obando y Bravo. Nicaragua's newspapers report, day after day, the jockeying among these powerful players: of dialogues, agreements, alliances, disagreements, rivalries, and fissures.

Nicaraguans wonder why they are so beholden to what are often called *caudillos*—strongmen—and why there is a culture in which those with authority seek every advantage, regardless of the circumstances or the impact on the nation-state. Why is it, for example, that Nicaraguan cabinet officials earn twice as much as their Costa Rican counterparts? Bolaños himself has been criticized. The monthly salary of 13,587 dollars that he receives is 357 times that of an agricultural laborer in Nicaragua. Moreover, as a former vice president, he is entitled to a monthly government pension of 7,000 dollars, which he initially collected. When criticized for accepting the pension while earning a government salary (together giving him a monthly income from the state of more than 20,000 dollars), Bolaños said, "It is not illegal." In time, faced with continuing criticism, he relented, but the incident reinforced a public perception that those who govern Nicaragua have been—and continue to be—indifferent to the national interest.

In the 2006 presidential election, the Liberal Party split, paving the way for the victory of Daniel Ortega. He received 38 percent of the vote (less than he garnered in 2001); together the two candidates from the Liberal Party received 55 percent, while two other candidates received the remaining votes. Ortega campaigned on a platform of peace and reconciliation, chose bright pink as the color of his campaign, and adopted for his jingle the melody of John Lennon's song "Give Peace a Chance." Ortega's detractors said it was all just *un show* (a show)—that Ortega is interested in power and that the country can only expect more self-interested "wheeling and dealing." Others wonder if, ironically, a strong, experienced leader like Ortega is essential for a catharsis of Nicaragua's governance.

Still, Nicaragua does have democratic institutions, imperfect as they may be. The country has a population of 5.5 million inhabitants (an estimate for 2005); however, Nicaragua has a professional army of only 14,000 soldiers. The country has the lowest homicide rate in Central America, even lower than that of neighboring Costa Rica. Despite political infighting, the economy is stable, with modest inflation. The country is poor, but natural resources abound, and the population is young and hard-working. Given all that they have suffered, many Nicaraguans feel that they are fortunate to still have a country. There is also the sentiment—or hope—that just as there are moments in the history of a country when there are only bad things (*cosas malas*), if this circle of ruination can be broken, good things (*cosas buenas*) can begin to happen.

CHOICES, CONSTRAINTS, IDIOSYNCRASIES, AND FORTUNE

In the 1950s and the 1960s, there was a flurry of thinking and writing in the academies of the United States, Canada, and Western Europe about how the poor countries of the world could catch up, develop, modernize. As European colonialism ended, many new countries were created, from mammoth India to archipelagos of tiny islands in the Caribbean like the Bahamas. These new countries had many evident needs. In response, there was a heady optimism, especially in United States academia, that the newly minted social sciences could guide a speedy transition from traditional society to modernity. A sense of urgency—and a source of funding—was provided by the tension between the United States and the Soviet Union, both anxious to have allies in the poorer parts of the world.

The apogee of this thinking and writing seems to have been the period between 1958 and 1966. Representative—and suggestive—book titles include: *The Passing of Traditional Society; Politics, Personality, and Nation Building; Old Societies and New States; Modernization: The Dynamics of Growth; Asian Drama: An Inquiry into the Poverty of Nations; The Politics of Modernization;* and *The Dynamics of Modernization.* Similarly, academic journals emerged with titles like *The Journal of Developing Areas.* This outpouring of books and articles came to be identified as a school, promoting modernization theory. The poorer countries of the world were seen as progressing on a continuum. On one end was traditional society, characterized by poverty, uneven national identity and weak levels of social organization, low levels of educational attainment and employment of technology, and governance by charismatic but capricious leaders. On the other end of the continuum was modernity. However, just what modernity meant remained surprisingly vague. It included at least economic prosperity and governance by institutions with social legitimacy. Perhaps unconsciously, though, modernity was equated with the life as lived in the prosperous countries of North America and Western Europe. At least initially, there certainly was faith in progress and a sense that all good things go together, that economic and political development go hand in hand, with prosperity leading to institutionalized democracy.

Mounting evidence, most dramatically from Africa, of the complexity (and in some instances the elusiveness) of development undermined the confidence in those who claimed to know the path to modernization. The war in Vietnam, the protracted—and bloody—independence movement in Algeria, and feisty regimes from Egypt to Indonesia that mocked the ideals of the United States and Western Europe also sapped consensus. In Latin America, the Cuban Revolution in 1959 stimulated the rise of guerrilla groups throughout the region that were keen on seizing control for the purpose of instituting radical social change. The armed forces in country after country responded ferociously, often sweeping aside civilian rule and governing themselves. Everywhere it seems, including on the pastoral campuses of North America and Western Europe, the mood changed.

A mortal blow to the intellectual viability of modernization theory came from within: in 1968, Samuel Huntington at Harvard University published *Political Order in Changing Societies*. He turned the thesis of modernization on its head, arguing that economic development occasions not democracy, but instead political conflict. For the most part, the voluminous works of the school, for all their earnestness, suddenly seemed naïve and were swiftly swept from bookshelves.

The countries of Central America, so near to the United States, were caught up in the intellectual and political currents of their powerful northern neighbor. The precepts of modernization infiltrated the thinking of aid officials from the United

States government as well as those with international financial institutions like the World Bank. Tension with the Soviet Union and fear of communism prompted the United States government to support a *coup d'état* in Guatemala in 1954. Similarly, the Cuban Revolution was the catalyst for the development assistance folded into the United States' Alliance for Progress. This assistance was delivered with the conviction flowing from the modernization literature that economic development leads to political development, understood at the time to be none other than republican government. As elsewhere, though, the import of the modernization literature faded. Indeed, the conflicts of the 1970s and 1980s made it seem other-worldly.

The end of the armed conflicts in Central America in the early 1990s and the embracing of the tenets of liberalism to guide economics and politics have contributed—along with other disparate trends—to Central America's de facto modernization, innocent of theory. However, just what is "modern" has changed since the benign years of the late 1950s and early 1960s when scholars in North American and Western Europe wrote copiously about poor countries. Modernity everywhere now conveys a decidedly mixed image: liberalism—the rights of individuals—as the dominant social paradigm; democracy as the reigning form of government; a waning interest in politics; markets driving economic decisions; evident but not contentious social cleavages; the rapid diffusion of information (including of "fashions" and "trends"); technological innovation; an extraordinary if often banal international trade in goods and services; consumerism, crime, travel, and migration (and a resulting stimulating mix of cultures); a shifting and unsettled fit between nation and state; economic uncertainty; and above all, constant change.

Central America is still poor, but it cannot be considered traditional. To be sure, there are backwaters—many of them—where life is little changed from previous decades. However, the prominent sectors of the region are quite modern, integrated—linked—to the world at large, including above all the United States. A Mexican intellectual, Jorge Castañeda, speaking about Latin America at large, claims that what is different

today between the region and the prosperous countries of North America—the United States and Canada—is just the relative size of the upper class, the middle class, and the lower class. Other differences, he concludes, are superficial. Surely, his judgment is too rash. Still, it is remarkable how Central American countries, in large part through their embracing of liberalism—of democracy and of unfettered markets—have modernized, have become integrated into the world, economically but also intellectually, politically, demographically, and culturally.

What do Central Americans make of this transition? Anabel González, an eminent lawyer who has negotiated many commercial agreements between her native Costa Rica and other countries, has clear views of the evolution of Central America. She is positive in her evaluation. "What," she asks, "would be—would have been—the alternative for these small, poor countries?" There is only one viable alternative in the world today for small countries: "integration." She has seen the hundreds of women entering and leaving the *maquilas* in San Pedro Sula, Honduras, and she has empathy for them. She knows their lives are hard. González asks, though, "What would be the alternative for them? Only the parcel planted with maize, the chickens, and the stray cow." "No," González says, pausing, "these are small, poor countries, and there is no alternative for them but to enter the world economy and to participate in its many markets. Central America's embracing of liberalism has brought many improvements." González brushes aside concerns about the cultures of the isthmus being overwhelmed by what flows into the region from abroad: "We have never had much to claim as our own; we are not like Mexico with its rich indigenous cultures. We are free to choose what we like from here and from abroad. This freedom is widely appreciated, and it is exercised every day."

González emphasizes that what comes from integrating into the world at large—and the world economy in particular—depends on the choices made within individual nation-states. The transformation of Central America since the turmoil of the 1970s and 1980s is five separate stories: Guatemala, El Salvador,

Honduras, Nicaragua, and Costa Rica. She stresses that there are opportunities for choices and that Costa Rica has chosen something different—something better—than what the other four countries of the region have elected. Costa Rica's choices—including notably participation in the advance of computer technology—are feasible in part by earlier decisions made in Costa Rica, such as the hefty investment in education. Concomitantly, Nicaragua's choices, she argues, are limited—restricted—because of the damage wrought by continued political conflict and now smothered by political oligopoly. All countries face constraints, but there are choices. Good choices can bring immediate benefits and augment future opportunities. Conversely, mistakes are costly, in large part because they curtail opportunities.

González' great worry is the migration of Central Americans. She concludes solemnly, "A country cannot expect to develop, to progress, when its principal export—its principal contribution to the world economy—is its own people. The massive flight of Central Americans from their nation-states is perverse and pernicious." The country in her mind is clear: El Salvador. But where go Guatemala, Honduras, and Nicaragua?

Many other Central Americans, including prominently intellectuals, are more skeptical, or at least cautious, in evaluating the course of the countries of the isthmus. A Costa Rican with a graduate degree from a Dutch university worries that it is easier for small, poor countries to import the vices of large, rich countries than it is to emulate their virtues. His pair of examples: El Salvador and Honduras are plagued by violent gangs inspired by the Crips and the Bloods of Los Angeles, while high technology is elusive in the two countries. There are the same complaints of decades past, too, of protectionism in rich countries, of the economic muscle of rich countries that gets flexed at the most inopportune moments for Central America. The international economy, dominated as it is by large, wealthy countries, is a constant constraint for small, poor countries like those of Central America. To import, you need to export. Access to markets is crucial, as is demand for exports. Foreign capital is important, too, for small, poor countries, which so often have trade deficits.

The more common concern, though, is that the benefits brought by modernization have not been shared by all Central Americans. A strong editorial was published in the December 21, 2004, issue of Nicaragua's leading newspaper, *La Prensa*: "Las dos Nicaraguas" (The two Nicaraguas). Some Nicaraguans, it said, live well: driving cars, chatting on cell phones, shopping in malls, watching cable television. They are not just comfortable, but they are linked—in a stimulating way—through many of their activities, including most conspicuously through their consumption, to the world at large. Other Nicaraguans, though, are not just poor but isolated, marginal, and so, seemingly, backward. Their lives are hard, and their life choices are limited. This dichotomy has a geographical overlap: the capital versus the countryside and a handful of provincial cities. (In Honduras there are two "capitals": Tegucigalpa—for politics—and San Pedro Sula—for business.) Indeed, Central America can sometimes appear (with the exception, perhaps, of Costa Rica) as a collection of city-states—even remote suburbs of Miami—superimposed over a quaint, bucolic countryside.

This disparity between rich and poor, the capital and the interior, is not new, and neither is the contrast between modernity and tradition. What is novel, and a subject of uneasy reflection in Central America, is the way in which the embracing of liberalism at the end of the twentieth century and the beginning of the twenty-first century has remade the nations and the states of the isthmus, and so transformed the nation-states, the collected entities known familiarly as countries. Salvadorans, for example, wonder what it means for a fifth of the population to live abroad and for the country to depend so heavily economically on remittances. The country is awash not just in imported goods but in novel customs and traditions. Easter celebrations now commonly include the Easter bunny bringing chocolate to the children. A humble but articulate Salvadoran was blunt: "We are being invaded. We are losing our identity. We are not this, and we are not that (*no somos ni una cosa ni la otra*)." He concluded, "The invasion has advantages and disadvantages. Much depends on whether or not you are prepared and know what you want."

The status of the many Central Americans who have left their countries is also an open question. The British historian E. J. Hobsbawm, writing in *Nations and Nationalism Since 1780: Programme, Myth, Reality,* suggests that "the idea of 'the nation,' once extracted, like the mollusc, from the apparently hard shell of the 'nation-state,' emerges in distinctly wobbly shape." Is he right? Even if the nationality of migrants is "wobbly," they can still make contributions, from financial to cultural, to their states of origin. Yet it appears unclear if these contributions, diverse as they are, strengthen or undermine the countries. Maybe both.

The literature on modernization was turgid, often opaque, and deterministic, but its concern with nations—the construction and maintenance of identities for large masses of people— and with states—composed of the institutions and norms of governance—has renewed import. Two tasks were always seen as paramount for countries: nation-building and state-building. These twin tasks were seemingly achieved long ago in Central America, if only imperfectly. However, countries are always under construction. A study of El Salvador organized and underwritten by Oxfam America concluded that the nation-state remains a vital entity in Central America but that the prevailing liberal doctrine, with its openness to global economic, political, social, and cultural forces, is a threat. Many in the isthmus share this fear. Honduras' widely respected cardinal, Óscar Rodríguez, offers consul. In a speech reported in the Honduran newspaper *Tiempo,* November 26, 2004, Cardinal Rodríguez said, speaking of Central America: "We in the region have to know what is at the core of our identity and what vision is leading us forward." Every nation-state has its idiosyncrasies, lives within constraints, is buffeted by fortune, but it nonetheless also has choices.

Reviewing the evolution of the five Central American countries at one particular moment in time, as they exited the twentieth century (sometimes called "the long century") and entered the twenty-first century, embosses certain conclusions about how best to study diverse parts of the world. What stands out above all is the formative force of the nation-state as a country and institutional expression. Countries are artificial; they are

peculiar social and political constructions. And most of the poor countries of the world—including those of Central America—are colonial artifacts, inventions of barely remembered Europeans. But once constituted, however "banged together," nation-states take on a life of their own, becoming the dominant arena for the collision of the disparate forces that shape economic development, social and political organization, and culture.

There is an expression in Latin America: *Cada cabeza es un mundo* (Every individual is a world of its own). The same can be said for countries. Each is unique—and complex. Moreover, just as Sigmund Freud persuasively insisted that much of our minds is inaccessible even to ourselves, so much of the workings of countries remains obscure. Contemporary scholarship on the make-up and course of countries likes to highlight the importance of political and economic elites, of their coalitions and agreements. But these analyses are often so true that they are tautologies. Elites are defined to be elites because they make decisions. But why, at any one moment, do some get to make key decisions? And how and why do they make their choices? With how much autonomy do they act? Moreover, how do we identify other variables within the cauldron of influences, from geography to class structure and conflicts to fashions in ideas? Just what is the weight of past decisions on the present? Can we even be sure of our abilities to pinpoint important choices and decisions in polities?

Our collective inability to answer these questions acutely is made embarrassingly evident by the failure to develop theories with any predictive utility. Countries, like the individuals they resemble, are capable of abrupt—unforeseen—shifts, of progress, stagnation, decline, self-destruction, and, even, metamorphosis. Guatemala, for example, is no longer the military garrison so long belittled by scholars. It changed. So have, over the past century, countries as varied as Chile, Ethiopia, Iran, Germany, Russia, and Japan. In other cases, such as with India, it is the durability of the extant regime that is confounding.

Looking closely at the five Central American countries not only reveals the daunting number of variables that shape a polity's destiny and the chaotic ways in which they interact with each other, but just how diverse even supposedly "similar" outcomes can be. There are as many dependent variables as independent variables. "Liberalism," "democracy," "market economy"—all are different from one country to the next. Indeed, the recent history of the Central American countries suggests that politics and economic activity can easily lead to outcomes that do not fit well into any established normative, ideological, or theoretical framework. Moreover, within any given country, grand philosophies and schemes for organizing politics and the economy—and their fruits—can gyrate erratically over time. A centenarian in Nicaragua would be most baffled by hearing, yet again, the word "liberal." Countries are always in flux; they are works in progress.

There is a continuing need for studies of individual countries and the comparative study of countries in particular geographical regions. Countries are relevant units of analysis. Empiricism is unavoidable; context matters. Labels, typologies, concepts, and models are seductive, but they must be used with a healthy sense of skepticism. They almost always need—at the least—to be qualified. The siren of parsimonious theory must be resisted, too. Comparisons are stimulating, and generalizations and propositions are always welcome. But it is best—and intellectually honest—to continue asking question after question, even if neat answers—or any answers—are elusive. Probing questions lead to an appreciation and an understanding of complexity.

PHOTOGRAPHY

Árbol ceibón, Tipitapa, Nicaragua, 1994. Celeste González.

Volcán Momotombo, Nicaragua, ca. 1930. Photographer unknown.

Chichicastenango, Guatemala, ca. 1930. Photographer unknown.

Haciendo tortillas, Costa Rica, ca. 1930. M. Gómez Miralle.

Comunidad indígena de San Lucas, Palacaguina, Nicaragua, 1993. Celeste González.

Última hilandera, Matagalpa, Nicaragua, 1988. Celeste González.

Payaso Firuliche, Managua, Nicaragua, 1986. Celeste González.

Carnaval, Matagalpa, Nicaragua, 1985. Celeste González.

El Rincón del Diablo, Chontales, Nicaragua, 1992. Celeste González.

Jovencitas de Somoto, Nueva Segovia, Nicaragua, 1996. Celeste González.

Poeta Carlos Martínez Rivas, Managua, Nicaragua, 1987. Celeste González.

Planta Empacadora Standard Fruit Company, Finca #6, Río Frío, Sarapiquí, Costa Rica, 1989. José Zúñiga.

Esperando camión, Matagalpa, Nicaragua, 1985. Celeste González.

Mata-palo, Ticuantepe, Nicaragua, 1991. Celeste González.

NOTE

Printed sources of data—quantitative and non-quantitative—are listed in the bibliography. In the text, institutions that are the source of data—usually published in compendiums—are identified by their English-language names. In the bibliography, though, all entries are in the language of the reference.

BIBLIOGRAPHY

MONOGRAPHS, PERIODICALS, AND WEBSITES

Achard, Diego, and Luis González. *Un desafío a la democracia: Los partidos políticos en Centroamérica, Panamá y República Dominicana.* San José: Banco Interamericano de Desarrollo (BID), Instituto Internacional para la Democracia y la Asistencia Electoral (IDEA), and Organización de los Estados Americanos (OEA), 2004.

Anderson, Benedict. *Imagined Communities: Reflections on the Origin and Spread of Nationalism.* London: Verso, 1983.

Banco Central de Nicaragua. *Informe anual 1977.* Managua: Banco Central de Nicaragua, 1978.

Bancroft, H. H. *History of Central America,* volume 1. San Francisco: History Company, 1890.

Binder, Leonard. "The Crisis of Political Development." In *Crises and Sequences in Political Development,* by Leonard Binder, James Coleman, Joseph LaPalombara, Lucian Pye, Sidney Verba, and Myron Weiner, 3–72. Princeton: Princeton University Press, 1971.

Carothers, Thomas. "The End of the Transition Paradigm." *Journal of Democracy* 13 (January 2002): 5–21.

Casas, Bartolomé de las. *The Devastation of the Indies: A Brief Account.* Baltimore: Johns Hopkins University Press, 1992. First published in Spain in 1552 as *Brevísima relación de la destrucción de las Indias.*

Colburn, Forrest. "The Left in Guatemala." *New Leader,* November/December 2000, 12–14.

———. "A Talk with Costa Rica's Ex-President." *New Leader,* September/October 2002, 11–13.

Colburn, Forrest, and Iván Saballos. "El impulso a las ventas externas no tradicionales de Costa Rica." *Comercio Exterior* 38 (November 1988): 1027–1032.

Colburn, Forrest, and Fernando Sánchez. *Empresarios centroamericanos y apertura económica.* San José: Editorial Universitaria Centroamericana (EDUCA), 2000.

———. *Individuos* versus *instituciones en las democracias centroamericanas.* San José: EDUCA, 2001.

Collier, David. "Overview of the Bureaucratic-Authoritarian Model." In *The New Authoritarianism in Latin America,* edited by David Collier, 19–32. Princeton: Princeton University Press, 1979.

Comisión Económica para América Latina y el Caribe (CEPAL). *Panorama social de América Latina 2002–2003.* Santiago: CEPAL, 2004.

———. www.cepal.org.

Cruz, Consuelo. *Political Culture and Institutional Development in Costa Rica and Nicaragua: World Making in the Tropics.* Cambridge: Cambridge University Press, 2005.

De Ferranti, David, Guillermo Perry, Francisco Ferreira, and Michael Walton. *Inequality in Latin America: Breaking with History?* Washington, DC: World Bank, 2004.

De Remesal, Antonio. *Historia general de las Indias Occidentales y particulares a la gobernación de Chiapas y Guatemala,* volumes 1 and 2. Guatemala City: Tipografía Nacional, 1932. First published in Spain in 1619–1620 under the same title.

Fernández, Nelson. "Pago a ex patrulleros: Más conveniente que convincente." *Inforpress Centroamericana,* August 27, 2004, 8–9.

Frente Sandinista de Liberación Nacional (FSLN). "Documento de las 72 horas." Managua, 1979. Mimeographed assembly report.

Gaddis, John Lewis. *The Landscape of History: How Historians Map the Past.* Oxford: Oxford University Press, 2002.

Grindle, Merilee. *Challenging the State: Crisis and Innovation in Latin America and Africa.* Cambridge: Cambridge University Press, 1996.

Gudmundson, Lowell, and Héctor Lindo-Fuentes. *Central America, 1821–1871: Liberalism before Liberal Reform.* Tuscaloosa: University of Alabama Press, 1995.

Gutiérrez, Roberto. "El 'nica' y el 'tico', según un 'nica.'" *Revista Conservadora* 8 (May 1964): 45–47.

Hobsbawm, E. J. *Nations and Nationalism Since 1780: Programme, Myth, Reality.* Cambridge: Cambridge University Press, 1990.

Inter-American Development Bank. *Sending Money Home: Remittance to Latin America and the Caribbean.* Washington, DC: Inter-American Development Bank, 2004.

Latin American Center for Competitiveness and Sustainable Development (CLACDS) of INCAE. "Central America as a Business Platform for Japanese Companies." Alajuela, Costa Rica, 2004. Mimeographed report for the Nomura Research Institute.

Latinobarómetro. "La costumbre democrática: Una encuesta de Latinobarómetro." *Nexos,* June 2003, 63–78.

Lehoucq, Fabrice. "Ambivalence in the Tropics: The 2006 Elections in Costa Rica." *ReVista* 5 (Spring/Summer 2006): 16–17.

MacLeod, Murdo. *Spanish Central America: A Socio-Economic History, 1520–1720.* Berkeley: University of California Press, 1973.

March, James, and Johan Olsen. *Rediscovering Institutions: The Organizational Basis of Politics.* New York: Free Press, 1989.

McCleary, Rachel. *Dictating Democracy: Guatemala and the End of Violent Revolution.* Gainesville: University Press of Florida, 1999.

Nicaragua, Gobierno de la República de. *Documentos de la historia colonial de Nicaragua: Recuerdos del centenario de la independencia nacional.* Managua: Tipografía Nacional, 1921.

Oficina Ejecutiva de Encuestas y Censos (OEDEC). *Anuario estadístico 1977.* Managua: OEDEC, 1978.

Oxfam America. *Estudio y análisis de los avances de gobernabilidad en El Salvador a 12 años de la firma de los acuerdos de paz.* San Salvador: Oxfam America, 2004.

Pereyra, Carlos. *Historia de la América Española,* volumes 3 and 4. Madrid: Editorial Saturnino Callejas, 1924.

Pérez-Brignoli, Héctor. *A Brief History of Central America.* Berkeley: University of California Press, 1989. First published in Spain in 1985 as *Breve historia de Centroamérica.*

Poitevin, René, and Alexander Sequén-Mónchez. *Los desafíos de la democracia en Centroamérica.* Guatemala City: Facultad Latinoamericana de Ciencias Sociales (FLACSO), 2002.

Programa de las Naciones Unidas para el Desarrollo (PNUD). *Informe sobre desarrollo humano 2004.* New York: PNUD, 2004.

———. *Segundo informe sobre desarrollo humano en Centroamérica y Panamá.* San José: Proyecto Estado de la Nación, 2003.

Pye, Lucian. "Identity and the Political Culture." In *Crises and Sequences in Political Development,* by Leonard Binder, James

Coleman, Joseph LaPalombara, Lucian Pye, Sidney Verba, and Myron Weiner, 101–134. Princeton: Princeton University Press, 1971.

Quesada, Juan Rafael, Daniel Masís, Manuel Barahona, Tobías Meza, Rafael Cuevas, and Jorge Rhenán. *Costa Rica contemporánea: Raíces del estado de la nación.* San José: Proyecto Estado de la Nación, 1997.

Revista de la Academia de Geografía e Historia de Nicaragua, volumes 1, 2, and 3. Managua: Academia de Geografía e Historia de Nicaragua, 1936, 1937, 1938.

Rodríguez, Florisabel, Silvia Castro Méndez, and Johnny Madrigal Pana. *Con la herencia de la paz: Cultura política de la juventud centroamericana.* Heredia, Costa Rica: Editorial Fundación de la Universidad Nacional (EFUNA), 2003.

Ruíz, Miguel. "El 'tico' y el 'nica', según un 'tico.'" *Revista Conservadora* 8 (May 1964): 47–49.

Salvatierra, Sofonías. *Contribución a la historia de Centroamérica: Monografías Documentales,* volumes 1 and 2. Managua: Tipografía Progreso, 1939.

Sánchez, Fernando. "Dealignment in Costa Rica: A Case Study of Electoral Change." Ph.D. dissertation, St. Antony's College, Oxford University, 2003.

Secretaría de Integración Económica Centroamericana (SIECA). www.sieca.org.gt.

Secretaría General del Sistema de la Integración Centroamericana (SG-SICA). *La integración centroamericana: Beneficios y costos.* San Salvador: SG-SICA, 2004.

Seligson, Mitchell, Annabelle Conroy, Ricardo Córdova Macías, Orlando Pérez, and Andrew Stein. "Who Votes in Central America? A Comparative Analysis." In *Elections and Democracy in Central America, Revisited,* edited by Mitchell Seligson and John Booth, 151–182. Chapel Hill: University of North Carolina Press, 1995.

Vega, Andrés, editor. *La colección Somoza: Documentos para la historia de Nicaragua.* Madrid: Imprenta Viuda de Galo Sáenz, 1954.

Weber, Max. *From Max Weber: Essays in Sociology.* Translated and edited with an introduction by H. H. Gerth and C. Wright Mills. New York: Oxford University Press, 1958.

Woldenberg, José. "Los partidos." *Nexos,* July 2000, 36.

Woodward, Ralph Lee. *Central America: A Nation Divided.* Second edition. Oxford: Oxford University Press, 1985.

World Bank. *The Economic Development of Nicaragua*. Washington, DC: World Bank, 1952. (The full report was published in 1953 by The Johns Hopkins University Press in Baltimore. It bears the same title but, at 424 pages, is much more detailed.)

———. *World Development Report 2005*. Washington, DC: World Bank and Oxford University Press, 2004.

Yashar, Deborah. *Demanding Democracy: Reform and Reaction in Costa Rica and Guatemala, 1870s–1950s*. Stanford: Stanford University Press, 1997.

Zavala, Silvio. *Contribución a la historia de las instituciones coloniales en Guatemala*. Guatemala City: Talleres de la Universidad de San Carlos, 1967.

Zerubavel, Eviatar. *Time Maps: Collective Memory and the Social Shape of the Past*. Chicago: University of Chicago Press, 2003.

NEWSPAPERS

La Nación (Costa Rica)
La Prensa (Nicaragua)
La Prensa Gráfica (El Salvador)
Siglo Veintiuno (Guatemala)
Tiempo (Honduras)

ABOUT THE AUTHORS

Forrest Colburn has a doctorate in government from Cornell University. His publications include *Latin America at the End of Politics*, published by Princeton University Press. Arturo Cruz has a doctorate in history from Oxford University. Among other works, he is the author of *Nicaragua's Conservative Republic, 1858–93*, published by Palgrave in its St. Antony's Series.